WHAT IS MY VALUE
INSTRUCTIONALLY
TO THE TEACHERS
I SUPERVISE?

ASCD MEMBER BOOK

Also by Baruti K. Kafele

BARUTI K. KAFELE

WHAT IS MY VALUE INSTRUCTIONALLY TO THE TEACHERS I SUPERVISE?

ascd

Arlington, Virginia USA

2800 Shirlington Road, Suite 1001 • Arlington, VA 22206 USA
Phone: 800-933-2723 or 703-578-9600
Website: www.ascd.org • Email: member@ascd.org
Author guidelines: www.ascd.org/write

Richard Culatta, *Chief Executive Officer;* Anthony Rebora, *Chief Content Officer;* Genny Ostertag, *Managing Director, Book Acquisitions & Editing;* Mary Beth Nielsen, *Director, Book Editing;* Liz Wegner, *Editor;* Georgia Park, *Senior Graphic Designer;* Cynthia Stock, *Typesetter;* Kelly Marshall, *Production Manager;* Shajuan Martin, *E-Publishing Specialist;* Kathryn Oliver, *Creative Project Manager*

PAPERBACK ISBN: 978-1-4166-3345-7   ASCD product #125032
PDF EBOOK ISBN: 978-1-4166-3346-4; see Books in Print for other formats.
Quantity discounts are available: email programteam@ascd.org or call 800-933-2723, ext. 5773, or 703-575-5773. For desk copies, go to www.ascd.org/deskcopy.

ASCD Member Book No. FY24-9 (Dec 2024 P). ASCD Member Books mail to Premium (P), Select (S), and Institutional Plus (I+) members on this schedule: Jan, PSI+; Feb, P; Apr, PSI+; May, P; Jul, PSI+; Aug, P; Sep, PSI+; Nov, PSI+; Dec, P. For current details on membership, see www.ascd.org/membership.

Library of Congress Cataloging-in-Publication Data

Names: Kafele, Baruti K., author.
Title: What is my value instructionally to the teachers I supervise? / Baruti K. Kafele.
Description: Arlington, VA : ASCD, [2025] | Includes bibliographical references and index.
Identifiers: LCCN 2024038117 (print) | LCCN 2024038118 (ebook) | ISBN 9781416633457 (paperback) | ISBN 9781416633464 (pdf)
Subjects: LCSH: Teachers—Supervision of. | Educational leadership. | School management and organization. | Teacher-administrator relationships.
Classification: LCC LB1777.5 .K34 2024 (print) | LCC LB1777.5 (ebook) | DDC 371.2/03—dc23/eng/20240821
LC record available at https://lccn.loc.gov/2024038117
LC ebook record available at https://lccn.loc.gov/2024038118

34 33 32 31 30 29 28 27 26 25   1 2 3 4 5 6 7 8 9 10 11 12

What Is My Value
INSTRUCTIONALLY
to the Teachers
I Supervise?

This book is dedicated to every principal and assistant principal out there striving to take their instructional leadership to higher levels of proficiency. As you do, the entire school wins.

Introduction

Is there a correlation between my supervision of teachers and their continued improvement of instruction?

It's game day in a high school football locker room on a Friday evening in September. The coaches have been preparing the team all week for the game and providing them with powerful messaging. The big day is now here. The team is excited, pumped, and ready to take to the field. But right before it's time to go out onto the field, the head coach gathers the team together for a final motivational message. After the message, he yells out, "Let's get this win!" The team responds with a loud "Let's go!" And as the team begins to run onto the field, the head coach yells, "Guys, if you need me or any of the assistant coaches, we'll be here in the locker room. Don't hesitate to come back and reach out to us." The players then run out onto the field to play the game, and the coaches remain in the locker room. Marinate in that one for a moment.

The head coach told the team to reach out if needed, but the implication here is that the coaches will not be on the field. The team is expected to go out onto the field, compete, and ideally win without the support of the coaches. Sounds a little absurd, right? In fact, I doubt that any of us have ever seen or heard of such a scenario. It's a given that the coaches will be on the sidelines and available to the team throughout the game. I repeat, *it's a given that the coaches will be on the sidelines and available to the team throughout the game.*

Just as it would be absurd for a team at any level to compete without being coached throughout the game, it's equally absurd for school leaders to "send teachers into the classroom to compete" without coaching them throughout the course of the school year.

The Problem and the Importance of Coaching

Far too many classrooms in U.S. schools are filled with countless uncoached teachers. Not every teacher hired is going to come in and be a superstar. All teachers, however, have the potential to be superstars. To maximize their potential, teachers need a mentor, a supporter, a nurturer—a coach. Every day that children are in the building is game day. Every day matters, and to get the most of each day, it is critically important that teachers are "coached up" *equitably*, as every teacher in the building doesn't need the same thing from you. Your data and observations will determine the degree of coaching each teacher requires. Under no circumstances should a teacher spend an entire school year in a classroom having only spoken to an administrator about teaching and learning during evaluation season; that would be unfortunate and detrimental to more children than imaginable.

Instructional Leadership and Instructional Coaching

Instructional leadership and instructional coaching are essentially job-embedded professional learning. They happen during the normal course of a regular school day. The coaches—the principal, assistant principals, instructional coaches, teacher leaders, and teachers—employ a peer-to-peer format. Beyond job-embedded professional learning, consider other sources of professional learning:

- Conferences
- Institutes
- Academies
- Seminars
- Lectures
- Presentations
- Podcasts
- Livestreams
- Videos
- Modules
- Books
- Journals
- Blogs
- Professional learning networks/social media

These sources of professional learning have one thing in common: They can't provide your teachers with direct feedback on a lesson. Think about it. You send a team of teachers to a conference, and they are blown away by the general sessions and keynote addresses. They are fired up and ready to take their students to great academic heights. They then go to the breakout sessions, and the information imparted has their heads spinning. They can't wait to return to school to implement everything that they learned. The thing is that although the teachers are recharged and rejuvenated, the keynoters and breakout session presenters won't accompany them to their classrooms to observe them implementing what they learned at the conference. Although attending the conference matters as a necessary first step, the follow-through—that is, the instructional leadership and coaching—brings it all full circle. That's why it's paramount that teachers share what they learned with administration and colleagues (as opposed to administration having no clue as to what teachers on their staff learned at a conference). Ideally, the teachers should bring back material that they can share and discuss with the administrators. The teachers should also share what they learned in staff meetings, PLCs, department meetings, grade-level meetings, and so on. Why not spread the wealth?

Leader Versus Leadership

During presentations, I frequently address the difference between the *leader* and the *leadership*. I tell my audiences that when I visit a school, I want to see the leadership without having to see the leader. I don't need the leader to be present for me to see, appreciate, or critique the leadership. The leader can only be in one place at one time. The leadership, on the other hand, should be omnipresent and ubiquitous and felt in every corner of the building.

When I visit a school on a regular school day, in addition to the principal's objectives for my visit, I focus on the following 12 areas where I want to see the leadership without having to see the leader:

- The overall culture of the building
- The overall climate of the building
- Alignment of the school with its mission
- Alignment of the school with its vision
- The level of positive energy in the building
- Staff morale
- Schoolwide systems

- Cleanliness of the building and grounds
- The overall leadership of the school
- The overall management of the building
- Equitable opportunities for students to grow, develop, and soar
- High-quality instruction

Although these areas are critically important and I pay a great deal of attention to them all, one thing is of paramount importance: high-quality instruction.

Where the Rubber Meets the Road

Instruction is where the rubber meets the road. As the primary purpose for children being in school is learning, instruction has to be on point. Although an uncoached teacher can be extraordinary, this book is not about *a* teacher. This book is about *all* teachers ensuring high levels of achievement for *all* children via job-embedded professional learning. Therefore, high-quality instruction must be the norm, and game-day coaching can never be undervalued. When I walk into a school and subsequently a classroom wishing to see the leadership without seeing the leader, in the case of instruction, I want to see the quality of the coaching via the productivity and performance of the teacher. I want to see that the culture of collegiality between administration and teachers is undeniable and ongoing throughout the school year.

Critical Questions Toward Driving the Work

To drive this work, it is important that you ask yourself these questions.

Why Do I Lead?

Although this seems like a simple and basic question, I've learned through years of asking principals and assistant principals that the answer can be quite complex, multifaceted, evolving, and downright complicated. As important as instruction is, in my early days as a young, new school leader, my "why" did not include instruction. The pressures and demands of my role, however, compelled me to quickly begin to look at instruction, to the point where instructional leadership became the purpose and primary nonnegotiable in all aspects of my leadership.

Are My Teachers at an Advantage *Because* I Am Their Leader?

Several years ago, I wrote a book entitled *The Teacher 50: Critical Questions for Inspiring Classroom Excellence* (2016). The first question in the book is "Are my students at an advantage *because* I am their teacher?" (p. 7). I considered this the quintessential question that teachers could ask themselves. Over time, I began to ask that question through a leadership lens: Are my teachers at an advantage *because* I am their leader? What I meant was whether there was something about the collegial relationship we shared that added value to the pedagogical development of the teacher. As a coach, the objective is for the teacher to continue to grow, develop, and evolve in the classroom. When that happens, the children win. The relationship between you and the teacher must be one where there's something advantageous to the teacher about your presence as a coach.

Does My Leadership Benefit My School *Academically?*

This question is the natural result of the previous question. You must regularly ask yourself whether your leadership benefits your school academically. At the end of the day, that is *the* question. Is there something about who you are as a leader in your school that increases the probability that your students will soar academically? That is what this leadership work must be about at its core.

Is My School a Better School *Because* I Lead It?

As I stated, I considered "Are my students at an advantage *because* I am their teacher?" the quintessential question that teachers should ask themselves. I soon after asked myself, "What is the quintessential question for myself as a leader relative to who I am instructionally?" Over time, I came up with the question "Is my school a better school *because* I lead it?" My response was in part rooted in who I was as an instructional leader. During my principalship, every day at dismissal, after the grounds were cleared of students, I would stare at the facade of the building and ask myself whether my school was better because I led it. I asked myself that question *every day*. My response was rooted in instructional leadership and student engagement—my two leadership nonnegotiables. In other words, regarding instructional leadership, I would reflect on and assess who I was on a given day as the instructional leader of my school. This internal conversation mattered to my practice as an instructional leader. Reflection and self-assessment provided me with a pathway to make adjustments and improvements when I was dissatisfied with my results—and I wrote the book *Is My School a Better School Because I Lead It?* (2019).

What Is My Value Instructionally to the Teachers I Supervise?

And now, with the title of this book, we've come full circle. For years as a presenter, while engaging an audience or group following the publication of *Is My School a Better School Because I Lead It?*, I would state, "If I ever come up with a question with as much or more potency, I will write a book based on it." Well, now, many years later, I have my new quintessential question. Let's break it down:

- **What is my value:** In other words, I'm asking, What is your worth? Does your leadership add value?
- **Instructionally:** I'm not asking what your value is to the teachers you supervise. Instead, I'm asking you what your value is *instructionally* to the teachers you supervise. What about your presence in your building makes teachers better . . . instructionally?
- **To the teachers I supervise:** I am not asking about every teacher in your school. Rather, I am asking specifically about the teachers who report to you, the teachers you supervise, the teachers with whom you work the closest.

If children are going to learn at optimal levels, instruction must be superior. As indicated earlier, professional learning can occur in various ways, but the professional learning teachers engage with in real time is ongoing instructional leadership and coaching. Through this process, you must regularly gauge your value instructionally to the teachers you supervise while also striving to provide the highest level of value possible to the pedagogical practices of *every* teacher you supervise. Throughout this book, I discuss exactly what that might look like in your school.

Questions Around Which the Book Is Structured

I developed the following framework of 10 self-reflective questions to help break down the answer to the question posed in the title of this book:

- What is instructional leadership, and what does it mean to my practice as a school leader?

- Do I understand that my main priority is student achievement and the continued improvement of instruction?
- Would I consider the instructional aspect of my leadership my primary focus as a leader, and what is the evidence?
- What does instructional leadership look like for me during a typical day?
- Do I have a philosophy, beliefs, opinions, and ideas about how children learn based on my own research, reading, and experiences?
- What is the significance of the pre- and post-observation conversation, including the analysis of data, to my leadership instructionally?
- What do I know about excellent pedagogy beyond who I was as a classroom teacher?
- What is the role of my administrative leadership team in establishing a culture of instructional leadership?
- How am I using my instructional coaches, and what measures have I put in place for them to be optimally successful?
- How do the teachers I supervise perceive me as an instructional leader?

This book comprises 10 chapters, each of which will address one question, and a Conclusion that will address a culminating question: Can I in good conscience refer to myself as an instructional leader in my school?

A Question to Keep at the Forefront of Your Mind

I encourage you to keep this question at the forefront of your mind every day as you lead: "Is there a correlation between my supervision of teachers and their continued improvement in instruction?" To make the point, let's take a journey:

During your years as a teacher, you had a notion that you could succeed as a building principal. Over time, you were increasingly convinced that what you were doing in the classroom was transferable to the building level with you as the assistant principal or even the principal. You felt that you could have an impact on far more students as a school leader. You enrolled in graduate school, simultaneously working extremely hard to earn your degree and certification and produce the intended results in your classroom.

After you graduated, you began interviewing for an assistant principal position. Although you failed to land a position after countless interviews, you kept pushing because you were convinced that as an assistant principal, you would make a difference. When you were finally offered a position as an assistant principal, you thought that you were ready to make your vision of larger-scale student success your new reality.

Shortly after beginning your tenure, you discovered that, under your principal, instructional leadership would be your secondary, or even a tertiary, responsibility. You went from being a phenomenal classroom teacher to a full-time disciplinarian who was also responsible for cafeteria duty and bus duty. The skills that you developed in the classroom were being used minimally. You determined that the principalship was your bigger picture and you would endure the assistant principalship for two years.

After two years as an assistant principal, you began interviewing for a position as a principal. Once again, countless interviews without landing a position. You interviewed unsuccessfully for the next three years. At that point, you'd been out of the classroom for five years, and despite being discouraged, you kept pushing. When a district finally offered you a position, you were elated and ready to make your vision of five years earlier your new reality.

After some time in the position, you realized that you had much to learn and a great deal on your plate. Your knowledge and understanding of principal leadership were limited. Your new reality was downright overwhelming. You put in 60-plus-hour weeks and worked weekends. The job took an emotional toll on you. Although the first year of the principalship was overwhelming and you wondered if that was really what you wanted to do with your life, you pushed through the first year.

As the year wound down and you began to reflect on your first year as a principal, you fixated on your reason for pursuing the principalship eight years earlier. You knew that your skill set as a teacher was transferable to building leadership and that your instructional success in the classroom was transferable to instructional leadership success at the building level. However, after a year as a principal, there is no evidence that the skills were transferred.

The Nonnegotiable Correlation

I'm sure that many of you reading this book will be able to identify with that journey, which brings me to the question that I refer to as the *nonnegotiable correlation*: "Is there a correlation between my supervision of teachers and their continued improvement in instruction?" That is, your teachers should be improving instructionally as a result of your collegial relationship with them. If they're not, self-examination of your leadership must become a priority.

The Positive

In the journey outlined, it's understandable that the individual, having had minimal exposure to school leadership as an assistant principal, initially struggled as a principal. There's a definite learning curve. In the scenario, neither the correlation nor the instructional leadership existed at the beginning of this leader's career. The positive is that this leader doesn't lose sight of their purpose and, hence, reflects on the year to determine what measures need to be taken moving forward.

Instruction Must Be Central

Whatever the stage of your career/leadership journey, the core of your leadership must be instruction. Everything else is secondary to instruction. If your daily duties do not allow you to be the instructional leader that your students and staff need you to be, you have ongoing adjustments to make. The intent of this book is to guide you in those adjustments so that at the end of the day, you know definitively that there is a correlation between your supervision of teachers and their continued improvement in instruction.

What's Inside

As with all of my books, I am writing in the second person—directly to you. This book, in addition to the aforementioned questions, is replete with more than 100 self-reflective, self-assessment questions to prompt you to look deeply within yourself as a leader regarding a variety of topics around instructional leadership and coaching. It is my hope and desire that, as you reflect on and assess the value instructionally that you bring to the teachers you supervise, your instructional leadership and coaching will continue to improve.

A Word About the Book Title

My use of the word *supervise* in the book title—and throughout the book—is extremely intentional.

I'm sure that some may think *lead, coach,* or *mentor* would have been more palatable. I considered and struggled with all three. I struggled because, when it comes down to it, you are as a school administrator accountable for the pedagogical proficiency of the teachers you *supervise*. In the administrator–teacher relationship, you lead, coach, and mentor your teachers. But at your core relative to your employment, you are the direct supervisor of your teachers—their evaluator of record—and that language can never get lost. And because of that language, you will be held accountable for your supervision of teachers, which includes supervising your teachers instructionally. It is with that understanding that I wrote this book.

1

Everything Else
Is Secondary

*What is instructional leadership, and what does it
mean to my practice as a school leader?*

O f all aspects of school leadership, instructional leadership
and coaching are without a shadow of a doubt the most
fascinating to me because they relate to the core reason that students walk into school every day: to learn. There
is a direct correlation between the quality of instruction and
intended student outcomes.

It's cliché to conclude that academic outcomes in schools
in high-poverty areas will be significantly lower than schools
in suburban districts. I don't subscribe to that way of thinking.
As an urban educator for 21 years who's lived in urban areas for
60 years, I completely understand the challenges of education
in urban areas. I believe that despite the challenges, obstacles,
experiences, realities, pressures, and demands of urban and rural
life, children can excel and compete with their suburban peers.
However, the road to academic prosperity in urban and rural
schools differs from that in suburban schools. The challenges
are such that I could easily write a book that details how to

resolve them. My purpose here is to discuss your role as instructional leader and instructional coach, the coaching that I likened in the Introduction to coaching a football team.

I find instructional leadership fascinating relative to what can result when it's implemented with fidelity. This can be quite challenging, particularly in urban and rural schools where the myriad challenges faced by students translate to behaviors that result in assistant principals, and sometimes principals, being relegated to disciplinarians.

It is well known and documented that I strongly contend that the assistant principalship is the most misunderstood and underutilized position in education. Picture this: An assistant principal in a low-performing urban or rural school who supervises X number of teachers and who, without visiting their classrooms for significant periods of time or providing input, gives the teachers glowing evaluations at the end of the year. Other than internal motivation, what would compel a teacher to improve when mediocrity is being rewarded despite the low academic performance of the school? Based on the assistant principal's evaluations, the teachers are doing great work, and the low academic performance is attributed to the school being in an urban or rural area. This strengthens the belief that urban and rural schools cannot compete with their suburban counterparts, and they're doing the best that they can under the circumstances.

The titular question of this book essentially asks, What is your value? *Value* is the key word in this question. I'm asking about your instructional worth, importance, and usefulness to the teachers you supervise. Whether you are the principal or the assistant principal, do your teachers benefit pedagogically from your presence in the building? Do you have a collegial relationship with the teachers you supervise, and do they benefit from it? Does this collegial relationship translate to continuous improvement in student outcomes? Does the culture of your school facilitate instructional leadership and coaching being welcomed by teachers?

As indicated in the title of this chapter, instructional leadership is primary—and everything else is secondary. Instruction is where the rubber meets the road. The children are in the school to learn, and for learning to occur at a high level, the quality of the instruction must be exceptional. Although a number of teachers in your building are extraordinary and need very little from you in terms of coaching, some need a great deal from you and others just a bit—more than enough to keep you mighty busy with the instructional aspect of your leadership.

Instructional Leadership Versus Instructional Coaching

As everything is secondary to instructional leadership, you can't afford to give it short shrift. To that end, the primary self-reflective question of this chapter is "What is instructional leadership, and what does it mean to my practice as a school leader?" It is a great starting point because I've learned through my travels that there is a considerable amount of confusion around the title "instructional leader." Although, as you will notice, I use "instructional leadership" and "instructional coaching" interchangeably, I want to distinguish between the two. What I mean by instructional coaching is the instructional conversations that you have with teachers, including follow-up classroom visits and post-visit feedback conversations, or the *micro* aspect of who you are instructionally. Instructional leadership, on the other hand, is your overall capacity to lead the teachers you supervise instructionally, or the *macro* aspect of who you are instructionally, which I'll unpack throughout this book.

What It Means to Be an Instructional Leader

The 10 primary areas that relate to what it means to be an instructional leader are as follows.

Instructional Leadership Is an Ongoing Focus on Coaching the Teachers You Supervise Instructionally, Including Maximizing the Time You Spend in the Classroom Observing Teaching and Learning

I want you to ask yourself this question: "To what extent am I an instructional coach to the teachers I supervise, and how frequently do I follow up my coaching with classroom observations and provide teachers with immediate feedback based on what I observed?"

This question, along with the others in this book, will serve as the pocket mirror that will allow you to self-reflect, self-assess, adjust, and improve—to see who you are as a leader. Do you spend sufficient time within your coaching capacity? Are you having one-on-one discussions on instruction with teachers? Are you conducting classroom visits? Are you following up with teachers in a timely manner to discuss what you observed?

I can hear some of you saying as you read, "Hold on, Principal Kafele. Discipline is real in my building. It's nonstop from the time the students enter the building until dismissal. Do you really think I can increase the time I give to instructional leadership with all that is on my plate?" My answer is yes. In Chapter 8, I will detail how. Throughout this book, I will also address those of you who may be saying, "But Principal Kafele, I am pulled in so many directions throughout the course of a day that it is hard to focus on instructional leadership."

Instructional Leadership Is an Ongoing Focus on the Academic Goals, Mission, and Vision of Your School

I want you to ask yourself this question: "To what extent do my school's academic goals, mission, and vision inform my instructional coaching and leadership?"

I have three follow-up questions for you: What are your school's aggregate academic goals for the current school year? What is your school's mission? What is your school's vision? I cannot overstate the importance of these three questions to your instructional leadership effectiveness. Your school's academic goals must drive your coaching. There can't be a disconnect between the goals of your school and the coaching that you provide. The two must be aligned. It would be futile to provide coaching that doesn't align with the school's goals.

Then there's the mission and the vision of the school. I've been to countless schools where no one in the building knows the mission or vision of the school, which I find quite disheartening. When folks reach for their phones to look on the website for the school's mission and vision after I ask what they are, I tell them not to bother. You either know them or you don't. But knowing isn't enough. You must live the mission and the vision, which should be known by *all*. When I was a principal, not a day went by without students standing and reciting the school mission and vision during morning announcements. I would also ask students to recite them when I ran into them in the hallways. The mission and vision were critically important to both the academic success of the school and my instructional leadership. (I will discuss the mission and the vision in more detail later in the book.)

I say all of this to get across that as instructional leader, your coaching must be rooted in your school's academic goals, mission, and vision. Do you know your school's aggregate academic goals and benchmarks? Do your teachers know your school's aggregate academic goals and benchmarks? Do you know your school's mission and vision? Do your teachers know your school's mission and vision? Do your school's aggregate goals, mission, and vision inform who you are as an instructional leader?

Instructional Leadership Is an Ongoing Focus on Your District's Curriculum and State's Content Standards

I want you to ask yourself this question: "To what extent do my district's curriculum and my state's content standards inform my instructional leadership and coaching?"

I am aware that there are various schools of thought regarding the significance of lesson planning—with some administrators deeming it extremely important, some considering it irrelevant, and others finding it somewhat important. Throughout my tenure as a principal and an assistant principal, I deemed it extremely important, and now, as an educational consultant, I still deem it so. Lesson planning allowed me to clearly see how teachers were addressing curriculum in their lessons. This mattered to me as an instructional leader. I knew curriculum, and I understood that it was the lifeblood of the academic process. As instructional leader, I had to ensure that teachers were addressing the state content standards to avoid "teaching to a test" as opposed to "teaching to the standards" (as there's a huge difference between the two). Are you conversant in your district's curriculum relative to your content areas? Are you conversant in your state's content standards relative to your content areas? Are your teachers conversant in your district's curriculum and state's content standards? As instructional leader, your ongoing focus on both is mandatory if your instructional leadership is going to add value to the teachers you supervise.

Instructional Leadership Is an Ongoing Focus on the Academic Program of Your School

I want you to ask yourself this question: "To what extent is the overall academic program of my school a priority of my leadership?"

This question is an extension of the question regarding district curriculum and state standards. I want you to consider the entire academic program of your school. Now take a look at yourself in your mirror and ask yourself to what extent the academic program of your school is a priority of your leadership. How familiar are you with the academic program of your school? To what degree are you involved and engaged in your school's academic program? To what extent does your school's academic program inform who you are as instructional leader? As instructional leader, your school's academic program must be a priority of your overall leadership inclusive of your instructional coaching.

Instructional Leadership Is an Ongoing Focus on Individual Student Academic, Attendance, and Discipline Data

I want you to ask yourself this question: "To what extent do individual student academic, attendance, and discipline data inform my instructional leadership and coaching?"

As instructional leader, your focus must be on *every* teacher you supervise and on the pedagogy of the teachers you supervise. However, while your teachers are in their classrooms, their focus is on the students, and that's where you come in. What is it about your instructional leadership that makes teachers proficient relative to individual student achievement? What is it about your instructional leadership that makes teachers proficient relative to student attendance? (In other words, what is it about teachers' presence—who they are as teachers—that compels students to want to be in school every day?) What is it about your instructional leadership that makes teachers proficient relative to student behavior? Improvement in each of these areas is rooted in the analysis of student data. What is being done with the data generated every second of the school day? Further, are your teachers comfortable with or proficient in data analysis? Although many decisions made throughout the course of a school day are emotion- or judgment-driven, other decisions must be supported by data. An important component of who you are as instructional leader must be informed by how you assist and support the teachers you supervise with analyzing and using student data and making data-informed decisions.

Instructional Leadership Is an Ongoing Focus on the Aggregate Academic, Attendance, and Discipline Data of Your School

I want you to ask yourself this question: "To what extent do aggregate academic, attendance, and discipline data inform my instructional coaching and leadership?"

Here, I want to review your role as it relates to aggregate data. As an instructional leader in your school, you must relentlessly focus on the aggregate data of your school. When we talk about the mission of the school academically, the mission of the school relative to attendance, and the mission of the school relative to discipline, that's aggregate data. Those three areas provide a snapshot of your school. How do your aggregate academic data inform your instructional leadership? How do your aggregate attendance data inform your instructional leadership? How do your aggregate discipline data inform your instructional leadership currently?

Instructional Leadership Is an Ongoing Focus on School and Classroom Culture

I want you to ask yourself this question: "To what extent does the prevailing culture of my school inform the amount of time and energy I devote to instructional leadership and coaching?"

You cannot be an effective instructional leader in a school with a culture that prevents you from being one. School culture is everything. It's the way that your school operates, functions, lives, and thrives. If your school's culture is not conducive to you spending a great deal of time coaching teachers and observing instruction, your abilities in those areas will be minimal or non-existent. That will translate to you squeezing once- or twice-a-year classroom visits during evaluation season into your schedule, which will do little to help average teachers become amazing teachers. Your school's culture must be a primary focus of yours as an effective instructional leader. To what extent is the culture of your school a leadership priority? To what extent do you and the other members of the leadership team strategize on culture? To what extent are you putting forth the effort to establish a culture of instructional leadership?

Instructional Leadership Is an Ongoing Focus on the Environmental Factors That Affect the Students in Your School

I want you to ask yourself this question: "To what extent do environmental factors that affect my students' lives inform my instructional leadership and coaching?"

I never allowed environmental factors to be an excuse as to why I couldn't be an effective school leader. I was aware of those factors before I took the job but concluded that I was the right person for the job to, as I worded it, "achieve the impossible." I didn't ignore the environmental factors, and neither should you.

They are a large part of your students' realities, and pretending that they don't exist is tantamount to malpractice. The environment outside the school walls matters and affects learning on multiple levels.

Consider students who live in areas where crime, gangs, and drugs are prevalent. As the environment can affect the students immeasurably, it can't be ignored. There may be teachers and leaders who have only a surface-level understanding of such areas, but the environmental reality of your students is a reality of your leadership. You can't use your students' realities as excuses for poor school and student performance. You must approach addressing these challenges through a lens that differs from that of your suburban counterparts. You must consider students' realities *your* realities, and you—and your teachers—must own and be informed by them. How are you being informed? What resources are you tapping into? What human resources are you tapping into? How is this information making its way to your teachers? What is your value to the teachers you supervise in this regard? Answering these questions is an important part of your growth and development as an instructional leader. Reading a textbook on instructional leadership is not the solution, as your students won't be found on the pages. You must tap into the people and resources that will help you nurture your professional growth, better serve your students, and understand the community in which your school is situated.

Instructional Leadership Is an Ongoing Focus on the Skill Sets, Experiential Backgrounds, Professional Growth, and Progress of the Teachers You Supervise

I want you to ask yourself this question: "To what extent do the skill sets, experiential backgrounds, professional growth, and progress of the teachers I supervise inform my instructional leadership and coaching?"

Teachers' skill sets must inform your instructional leadership. For example, when we think of equity in schools, we typically think of the students. But equity is also an important factor in your relationships with the teachers you supervise. Your teachers possess varying degrees of skill and, as an instructional leader, you can ill afford to forget that. Some teachers will need more from you than others. And veteran teachers can benefit from coaching, because research constantly reveals new ways to do things in the classroom as students change and evolve.

The experiential backgrounds of your staff relative to their work and personal lives are likely extremely diverse. This matters relative to who they are in their classrooms and has deep implications in how you approach them in your capacity as an instructional leader. There are teachers in your schools whose prior work or lived experiences have prepared them for success in your school. Conversely, there are teachers in your schools whose prior work or lived experiences may not be conducive to success in your school, and those teachers will need your leadership and support in ways that the aforementioned teachers may not.

As indicated in the Introduction, your instructional leadership is essentially job-embedded professional learning for your teachers. All other professional learning happens outside the classroom. Instructional leadership and coaching give teachers an opportunity to learn in real time on the job if the coaching, observation, and follow-up feedback occur in a short period of time. This is where you are an instructional leader and a professional developer.

I frequently ask school leaders what their comfort level is in surmising if teachers they supervise can conclude that they are better as a result of the collegial relationship that they have with the school leader. The most that a school leader could aspire to is that the work and the hours that they put in results in significant progress for teachers and gives them the opportunity to grow as instructional leaders. The goal must always be ongoing progress that is sustained over the course of the school year.

Instructional Leadership Is an Ongoing Focus on Your Professional Growth and Development and Determining How You and the Other Members of the Leadership Team Will Ensure That Teaching and Learning Occur at the Highest Levels

The final question I want you to ask yourself is this: "To what extent am I intentional about my own professional growth and development as an instructional leader?"

Although the sources of professional learning that I noted in the Introduction—conferences, institutes, academies, seminars, lectures, presentations, podcasts, livestreams, videos, modules, books, journals, blogs, professional learning networks/social media—are all good, they can't match the job-embedded professional learning that accompanies instructional leadership and coaching. As for your own professional learning, however, they must all be a part of your repertoire, including continuing to pursue advanced degrees in leadership. Your learning, which should emphasize instructional leadership and coaching, can never end.

2

My Instructional Leadership Wake-Up Call

Do I understand that my main priority is student achievement and the continued improvement of instruction?

Every book that I write includes snippets and vignettes of my experiences as a classroom teacher, an assistant principal, a principal, or a presenter. Because I am so passionate about the topic of instructional leadership, this chapter will be autobiographical. I will be brutally vulnerable, transparent, and authentic. I'll give you the good, the bad, and the ugly of my instructional leadership journey—which was not an easy one. I want to encourage those of you who are struggling in real time to become the instructional leaders you desire to be to stay the course no matter how difficult the journey may be. The benefits to your students will be immeasurable. When I hear the success stories of the students I had long ago, I know that all that I invested in my leadership played a role in the outcomes that they now enjoy.

Many of you reading this book are doing so because you're familiar with and support my work, as it aligns with your work or your aspirations. Those of you being introduced to me through this book may find the experience a little different. All of my books are infused with my authentic self, as for 14 years I lived and breathed this work as a principal in urban schools, and I want to share some of my experiences with you. I regularly share my challenges, deficiencies, flaws, and shortcomings on my Saturday morning AP & New Principals Academy livestream, but I will go a little deeper here.

It is my hope and intention that by devoting an entire chapter to my formative years—beginning with my internship and ending with my first year of principal leadership in the context of becoming an instructional leader—you will be able to relate to my story and find it relevant to you and your work as you strive to be the instructional leader your staff and students need you to be.

My Internship

The culmination of my two years in graduate school was my administrative internship. I was really excited about it because I would have an opportunity to be a quasi-administrator. My principal, Dr. Alease Griffith, gave me a number of responsibilities that included cafeteria duty. I couldn't do a lot of the hands-on things that she may have wanted me to because I was still teaching 5th graders full-time. But during my prep period, I was in that cafeteria feeling like I was the principal of the building. In the afternoon after school, for two or three days per week, the assistant superintendent for human resources, Dr. Kenneth King, would come by the school to meet with me in the conference room. Those meetings made it clear to me that administration was on the horizon due to the depth of the conversations about all things school leadership. Those meetings would culminate with a variety of assignments that Dr. King gave me. These two assignments stand out to me to this day:

- **District policy.** On one of his visits, Dr. King came by the school with two thick district policy manuals. He laid them on the conference room table and said he needed me to read them in their entirety and become familiar with them. This blew my mind because the sight of these two manuals was quite overwhelming. I burned the midnight oil and read them both because I was hungry. He subsequently quizzed me on some of the policies in our meetings. He taught me that, as a school leader, I was going to regularly make a ton of difficult decisions and that those decisions must be supported by policy. If the decision wasn't supported by policy, it probably wouldn't hold up if challenged by affected parties.

- **Labor union contracts.** Our district had multiple labor unions for just about every category of employee. I will never forget the day that Dr. King came to the school with a plastic bag. He emptied the bag and before me was a stack of little booklets. The booklets were the contracts of every labor union in the district, including the largest union—the teachers. He said he needed me to read and study the booklets to become familiar with every bargaining unit's contract. Although I was overwhelmed, I completed the task quickly. Once again, Dr. King taught me that, as a school leader, I was going to regularly make a ton of difficult decisions, including decisions about employee rights, and that those decisions must be supported by employment contracts. If the decision wasn't supported by a contract, it probably wouldn't hold up if challenged by affected parties. Dr. King was quite the stickler about administrators knowing district policy and union contracts.

In addition to district policy and contracts, he also said I needed to be very familiar with New Jersey state statutes and codes and special ed law. Once again, a whole lot to read and digest.

Student Achievement and Teachers' Continued Improvement in Instruction

Instructional leadership, instructional leadership, instructional leadership. Although it came up a ton in graduate school, in the environment in which I worked, I only saw administration—the assistant principalship—from a distance. I could not make the connection between what I was learning in graduate school and what I saw and experienced in the school every day relative to instructional leadership and coaching. This is not to criticize my supervisor, who happened to be an assistant principal. I'm just saying that as I worked in environments where assistant principals were pretty much disciplinarians, it was a challenge for me to reconcile the difference between what I was learning and what I saw and experienced. I was going through this graduate school program to one day soon become an assistant principal, an urban school disciplinarian. (In the back of my mind, though, I was going to successfully take my classroom teaching success along with me to assistant principal leadership.)

What altered my thinking was one of my after-school conversations with Dr. King during which he said to me (and I'm paraphrasing), "Mr. Kafele, when you become a school administrator, your primary purpose of your supervision of teachers will be student achievement and their continued improvement of instruction." The room fell silent, and the world stood still. This was not a conversation about cafeteria duty, bus duty, discipline, policies, or contracts. No. This was the conversation about where the rubber meets the road—instruction. Those words weren't spoken by a professor who I would never see again after graduation. They were spoken by, if I ever became a principal in that district, my future direct supervisor and then one-on-one mentor. But do you know something, reader? After initially being startled, I realized that I'd heard Dr. King loudly and clearly yet didn't "hear" him at all. In other words, his words were a wake-up call. I "knew," however, that when I became an assistant principal, I'd be disciplining students all day. I felt it in my spirit. Does this resonate with any of you?

Visiting a High School During My Internship

As an intern, I was required to spend a day at a high school. That day marked the turning point for my outlook on instructional leadership. A small group of us arrived at the school at pretty much the same time, and the principal was waiting for us at the front entrance—which stood out to me and later influenced me to position myself at the front entrance of my school in the morning to greet my students. We soon went to the principal's office, where he briefed us on what the day would look like. In summary, he said we would visit classrooms and observe instruction.

As we approached the first classroom, before we walked in, he told us everything we were about to see instructionally. I found it odd that he would have such a degree of familiarity with a classroom before walking in, but once we entered, it was clear that he knew this classroom. After a few minutes, we debriefed in the hallway. I was amazed at the principal's knowledge of what was going on in that classroom, but the cynic in me thought that maybe he was just prepared. The rest of the morning mirrored the first classroom visit. We visited approximately seven classrooms that morning, and prior to walking into every classroom, the principal informed us of what we were about to observe instructionally—which was mind-blowing to me at that stage of my educational career. Clearly, the principal's knowledge of those classrooms went far beyond preparing for our visit.

After the classroom visits, we returned to the principal's office and had a conversation about instructional leadership that enabled me to fully make sense of the morning we'd had. He knew those classrooms because his influence was in those classrooms. His leadership instructionally was in those classrooms. That his relationships with the teachers in those classrooms was collegial, which translated to the school being a high-performing urban high school in New Jersey, was more than evident. I left that building fired up saying to myself, "I want to be that guy one day."

That one morning prepared me for instructional leadership more than grad school did in two years.

Assistant Principal Kafele, the Disciplinarian

I visited the aforementioned high school in April of 1996. In the year that followed, I was appointed assistant principal of an urban middle school in the district in which I'd taught. It would have happened a year earlier had I not been named County Teacher of the Year (in New Jersey, if you leave the classroom to go into administration the same year you are selected County Teacher of the Year, you have to forfeit the selection, and that I was not willing to do).

I'd been a 5th grade teacher in the same district until December of 1997. December 23, 1997, was my last day as a 5th grade teacher, and January 2, 1998, was my first day as a middle school assistant principal—and I remember that day as if it were yesterday. Disciplinary referral after disciplinary referral on day 1. On my first day on the job, I was either assigning students to detention or suspending them. And that was my life for the remainder of the school year. What an introduction to school leadership! I thought to myself, "This is not what I signed up for."

When the 1998–99 school year began, I vowed that I would become the instructional leader that I conceptualized that I could be. One of my challenges, however, was that I was (to be brutally honest) being used by my principal as a full-time disciplinarian. As he saw that as my role, I had to unilaterally figure out how to get out of the disciplinarian, cafeteria duty, teacher supply order clerk rut in which I found myself. And, to some degree, I did. I started to take the initiative on activities and programs that affected the culture of the school, which freed me up to devote time to the real work—that of instructional leader. But prior to those initiatives, there was nothing about my work that translated to instructional leadership. It simply wasn't a part of my reality. I was both frustrated and wished to return to the classroom *and* excited about the prospects that I continued to believe were on the horizon for me as a principal one day. I'm talking to someone out there.

Principal Kafele's Wake-Up Call

On the last day of the 1998–99 school year, I found out I was a finalist for principal of the school where I was the assistant principal. I landed the position days later. Whew! I was ready to now become the instructional leader that the principal I encountered during my internship was—or so I thought.

I quickly discovered that, as it related to being a brand-new principal, I had much to learn. I had my hands (and feet) in everything. And my new assistant principal (Kevin Booker, a former middle school teacher) was just as green and raw as I was. Kevin and I became great friends, allies, confidants, and comrades, and we learned together—one day at a time. Always within me was the desire to be an instructional leader. But my leadership aspirations were not aligned with my leadership reality. Now understand that I did in fact get into classrooms; I was in them regularly. However, the visits were not in any way rooted in collegial instructional leader–teacher relationships. I was just simply popping in and observing instruction. I only gave feedback where I saw issues and concerns that required immediate attention. But in terms of being in those classrooms as an instructional leader in that first year, I wasn't. I was securing information for evaluations and familiarizing myself with the classrooms and instruction but not necessarily helping teachers become better. I felt that I didn't have the time in the way I am going to explain fully later in this book.

As I reflected on it later, the question that I always had for myself was "What is the sense in visiting classrooms regularly if I'm going to hoard all of the information without using it constructively to help teachers to grow pedagogically?" In keeping with being vulnerable and transparent, in my mind during that year, I felt that my pop-in visits alone were in fact having an impact on instruction. That's called being visible and being present. Well, I thought my visibility and presence were going to be a game-changer, and as we approached state standardized testing season, I was feeling pretty good about the prospects for my year 1 assessments.

We took those assessments in March. I had to wait three months to receive our results, and when I did, I was crushed. Our scores were already low, but now they were lower. My head was spinning. I questioned whether I belonged. I wondered if my place was actually in the classroom. I wondered whether I mattered. I wondered if I was all talk. I wondered if the district still valued me. I wondered if I was built for the work. And then, to add insult to injury, my internship mentor, who was now my direct supervisor and my evaluator of record, called me and requested that I report to his office to discuss the test scores. OUCH!

When I arrived at Dr. King's office, he had the report of my school's scores on his desk. He asked me what happened. I proceeded to tell him how hard I worked, about the 60-hour work weeks and 16-hour weekends totaling 76-plus hours in the school per week. He responded to me saying, "I'm not questioning how hard you work. I'm questioning how smart you work." That stung for quite a while, but it served as my launching pad to instructional leadership. As much as it stung, I needed it. It was my wake-up call. At the core of my work as a school leader must be instruction. Said differently, it made concrete for me that "my main priority is student achievement and the continued improvement of instruction." I was now on the journey to true instructional leadership.

That's enough about me. Let's now zero in on you and, as we do, you will gain an understanding of the instructional leader that I became.

3

Where the Rubber Meets the Road

Would I consider the instructional aspect of my leadership my primary focus as a leader, and what is the evidence?

In Chapter 2, I posed the question "Do I understand that my main priority is student achievement and the continued improvement of instruction?" Children walk through your entrance doors to learn, but the learning goes far beyond content areas. Think of learning as a destination.

As I write, the National Basketball Association (NBA) playoffs are in full swing, and arenas are filled to capacity. Twenty thousand-plus fans are in those arenas rooting for their teams. Let's look at how the fans arrived. If they drove cars or SUVs, there were countless different makes, models, colors, price ranges, and years of manufacture based on preference, need, price, and circumstance. But some didn't drive at all. Some used a ride-sharing app, some took a taxi, some took public transportation, some rode with friends or family, and a small percentage may have even walked if they live in a big city and near the arena. My point then is that different fans used different means to get to the same place to see the same game. In the context of the game, the vehicle or means to get them there was never the end goal. The end goal was attendance at the game and, to go a step further, for their team to win the game. "What's this got to do with this chapter?" you may wonder. Everything!

Just as there are many modes of transportation to get to a destination, there are many modes of learning to get students from the proverbial Point A to the proverbial Point B. The effective teacher will determine how each child learns in the classroom and teach accordingly. Your role in all of this as the instructional leader is to assist the teacher in helping all students get to their destinations—learning, at a high level. To that end, consider the following questions:

- Have I deemed instructional leadership and coaching priorities of my leadership?
- How have I gone about prioritizing instructional leadership?
- Do other aspects of my leadership prevent me from being the instructional leader my staff and students need me to be?
- How would I rate my skill at planning, organization, and time management?
- Who are the other instructional leaders on my team, and what does our *collaboration*, *coordination*, and *cohesion* look like?
- Am I confident that my leadership team members are the instructional leaders I need them to be?
- In what ways do I hold my leadership team accountable for being effective instructional leaders?
- To what extent does our prevailing school culture prevent me from being the instructional leader I need to be?

Let's look at each question separately.

Have I Deemed Instructional Leadership and Coaching Priorities of My Leadership?

I want you to reflect on who you are or who you have become as a school leader. First, reflect on why you pursued school leadership. What was your reason for pursuing school leadership? What were your goals and objectives as a school leader? What was your vision of who and what you would become as a school leader? Was student learning at the core of your purpose, goals and objectives, and vision? Were instructional leadership and coaching at the core of your purpose, goals and objectives, and vision?

Let's look at you today. Are you leading within a purpose of student learning? Are you leading within goals and objectives of student learning? Are you leading within a vision of student learning? When you reflect on what your days in your school look like, do your actions reflect and support student learning? Who are you as a leader relative to student learning? Have you deemed instructional leadership and coaching priorities of your leadership?

Let's say, hypothetically, that when you were pursuing school leadership, your focus was instructional leadership and coaching, but the reality of the work shifted your focus and, consequently, instructional leadership and coaching took a back seat. That means that your reality as a leader must shift if teachers are going to be able to benefit from being coached by you.

Let's work our way through the questions to determine how you are going to make this shift your new reality.

How Have I Gone About Prioritizing Instructional Leadership?

In addressing this question, I'm thinking about the schools I have visited where there is chaos and confusion in the building, and the administrators and security spend the day running around putting out fires. We know that there's no way that the students in those schools are learning at high levels. Yes, there are a few breakthroughs, but as a school, the challenges are enormous. If you can relate to this scenario in any way, I ask you, How have you gone about prioritizing instructional leadership? The key word in this question is *prioritizing*. There are obvious issues in this school surrounding its overall climate and culture, but I want you to consider the number of incidents and infractions with origins in classrooms. Imagine, if you will, a teacher whose lessons neither engage students nor serve as vehicles to learning. That in and of itself is a recipe for classroom and school disaster. If that is the reality of the classroom, it is safe to anticipate and expect that you will be putting out fires over the course of an entire school year. Now tally up the number of classrooms in your school where there are teachers who need instructional coaching from you but you are unable to function in that capacity. It's then safe to assume that you've been preoccupied with noninstructional concerns throughout your building.

Instructional leadership must be made a priority. You must be intentional about putting instructional leadership first while strategizing ways to minimize any and all distractions and interruptions that are impeding your efforts to become the instructional leader your school demands you be. Remember, those incidents and infractions are happening in your absence as a coach and observer of your classrooms. Imagine if you had a collegial relationship with teachers while having an instructional presence in the classroom. It would make a tremendous difference.

Do Other Aspects of My Leadership Prevent Me from Being the Instructional Leader My Staff and Students Need Me to Be?

Given everything that has been written thus far about disruptions, distractions, and interruptions, this one is a no-brainer. If your classrooms are not functioning in ways that keep students inspired and engaged, there are going to be disruptions in the learning process. Said differently, if your teachers are not functioning in ways that keep learning relevant and relatable, there are going to be disruptions in the learning process. To that end, let's examine your day. Are you the instructional leader and coach your staff need you to be? If not, why not? If yes, you're on the right path.

Are the administrative aspects of your work keeping you from being the instructional leader your staff and students need you to be? My response is that you've got to prioritize the work. School leadership is not a 9-to-5 job. My position has always been that once your students are in the building, administrative work is secondary. That means I devoted my attention to the administrative work before students arrived and after they left, but once the students were in the building, it was all about students and staff, with a particular emphasis on instructional leadership.

Is student discipline keeping you from being the instructional leader your staff and students need you to be? My response is that student discipline is a climate and culture issue. Addressing discipline is a micro issue, but when there are countless disciplinary issues in a building, it becomes a macro issue that speaks to the culture of the building. It is typical to expend energy on the micro issue—discipline—while completely ignoring the macro issue—culture. Just as discipline typically receives a great deal of attention from administration, culture wants some love, too. It wants administration's attention, and when it doesn't receive it, the entire school community is adversely affected.

Is returning phone calls during the day keeping you from being the instructional leader your staff and students need you to be? My response is that you have to shift the culture in this regard. Responding to telephone calls throughout the day while the students are in the building can never be a priority. Yes, I understand that parents have legitimate concerns that in some cases need to be addressed immediately. But if parents are calling you throughout the day and you are responding to calls, your school in general and your instructional program in particular will suffer. You must instead set up a routine or system that begins with you explaining your role as instructional leader to parents during your back-to-school orientation or open house. Trust me when I tell you that many will be unaware that the role exists. Parents see you as the boss, which in their eyes translates to you always being available to them. You must detail your priorities and explain why they are your priorities so that parents understand your role. Parents should know that if you are always available because of an ongoing open-door policy, you are not engaged in the work that matters most—positioning yourself as an effective instructional leader so that their children's potential will be maximized. You have to put a system in place that allows you to be who you need to be in your school every day instead of answering phone calls all day (e.g., you can tell parents to leave you a message for nonessential calls and to call the secretary directly for essential calls).

The bottom line is that parents must gain an awareness and understanding of your primary focus of student achievement and the continued improvement of instruction. Many of your parents may not fully understand your roles based on their experiences as children. That means they still may not know the intricacies of principal and assistant principal leadership as adults. It is your job to explain it to them.

Is cafeteria duty keeping you from being the instructional leader your staff and students need you to be? If you are a principal, I will give you one lunch period per day to be in the cafeteria. Anything more is too much. You are the principal, and you have many important things to do beyond cafeteria duty. If your school has multiple lunch periods, rotate periods of supervision so that you're able to see all of your students over the course of a week. That time can be very productive if you are engaging with students as opposed to watching over them. If you are an assistant principal, I will allow you no more than two periods. Like the principal, your time is far too valuable for you to be engaging in cafeteria duty. Instructional leadership must be your priority—particularly if you are in a low-performing school. How does your school shift its trajectory if you have little to no involvement with what is happening in classrooms relative to teaching and learning? My response: The trajectory is not going to shift. Spending multiple periods in a cafeteria is an absolute waste of the resource called assistant principal leadership. If you have to supervise a cafeteria because it's disorderly, you must address the issue of cafeteria culture, and that will not be addressed or rectified by you standing over children for multiple periods. The culture, including your cafeteria systems and procedures, requires attention.

Are staff concerns keeping you from being the instructional leader your staff and students need you to be? My response is it is always healthy when staff know they have access to leadership. However, as a school leader who prioritizes the instructional aspect of the work, you can't spend entire days addressing staff concerns. Once again, you must put systems in place that allow you to maximize the amount of time you will spend on instructional matters while ensuring that all staff concerns are being addressed in ways that minimize keeping you from the instructional aspect of your leadership.

How Would I Rate My Skill at Planning, Organization, and Time Management?

School hours are, give or take, the proverbial 8 to 3. That means you have only 7 hours per day and 35 hours per week to make magic happen instructionally at your school. In the grand scheme of things, that is not a lot of time. If your job description had one item only and that was instructional leadership, then one could argue that 35 hours per week is sufficient. But the fact of the matter is that you have a great number of responsibilities—endless responsibilities, countless responsibilities—that can seem overwhelming. Heck, the contents of this book can seem overwhelming, to be quite honest.

This translates to the need for you to be quite adept at *daily* planning, organization, and time management. Notice that I included the word *daily*. School days are too complex, too challenging, for you to rely on annual school-level planning. No. You must be detail-oriented. That will require that your days be well thought out and planned with an emphasis on the instructional aspect of your leadership. Your days must also be organized. With the stakes being as high as they are, you can't lead haphazardly. Your day must be structured, arranged, and systematic. This cannot be overstated if you are going to be the instructional leader your students and staff need you to be. Lastly, you must be a master at managing and protecting your time. If you fail to do so, as the saying goes, your time will manage you.

With all this being said, how would you rate your skill at planning, organization, and time management? Are your days thoroughly planned out, or do you simply show up and wait for the stimuli to come at you? Are your days structured and organized, or are you all over the place within your leadership? Do you effectively manage your time, or does your time manage you?

Who Are the Other Instructional Leaders on My Team, and What Does Our *Collaboration*, *Coordination*, and *Cohesion* Look Like?

The leadership team typically comprises the principal, assistant principals, instructional coaches, and, in some cases, teacher leaders. These entities have instructional leadership and coaching in common. I have seen cases where the functioning of this group as a team stops at the word *team*. In other words, they are just a group of leaders who have categorized themselves as leadership team members, but they do not function as a team in the true sense of the word.

When the leadership team functions as a team, there's synergy. The key components for creating synergy are the team's sense of collaboration, coordination, and cohesion. This requires intentionality. The principal brings the team together and leads the effort to have members share their purpose, goals and objectives, mission, and vision and what their work will look like, while also keeping in mind that a toxic culture within the team or the school can sabotage their intentions and efforts. This translates to the need for the team to clearly understand its function relative to leadership in general and instructional leadership in particular. The ongoing collaboration, coordination, and cohesion of the team must be an ongoing priority.

Am I Confident That My Leadership Team Members Are the Instructional Leaders I Need Them to Be?

This question is actually an extension of the previous question. The key parts in the question are "confident" and "I need them to be." In other words, this is *your* team and, as leader of your team, your ability to be confident in them is nonnegotiable. How the team functions is a reflection of your leadership. No two leaders, leadership teams, or schools are alike. Every leader, every team, and every school faces challenges and obstacles and has needs, interests, and priorities, hence the wording, "I need them to be."

As you lead, you have your own instructional purpose, mission, and vision. When I was a school leader, I had my own instructional purpose, mission, and vision. Your instructional purpose, mission, and vision may or may not align with those of the other principals in your district, and that's OK. You are who you are. To that end, you must be able to develop your team around *your* leadership purpose, mission, and vision with the assumption that at the core is student achievement and the continued improvement of instruction. As you develop your team, you must simultaneously develop the confidence that they will be able to function in alignment with who you are and what you expect as the leader of your school and the leader of your leadership team. As a team, you must be on the same page relative to each of your roles as instructional leaders. You don't all have to see the world the same way, but there must be commonality around how you approach instructional leadership.

Getting along with one another and having great camaraderie as a team is good and necessary—but it's not enough. A common purpose, mission, and vision of instruction must drive the leadership team and the overall instructional program of your school. And as leader, you must ultimately be confident each member of the team will be of high value to the teachers they supervise instructionally, without you having to constantly monitor and oversee the performance of the members of the team. You are the leader and must therefore set the tone for your leadership team to grow, develop, and evolve into the instructional leadership team that will take your school to heights previously unimagined.

In What Ways Do I Hold My Leadership Team Accountable for Being Effective Instructional Leaders?

In a well-functioning instructional leadership team, each member of the team coaches a percentage of the teaching staff with you, the principal, coaching your own portion of the teaching staff. The difference between you and everyone else on the team is that you are being held accountable by your superiors, your local board of education, and your parents and community for every teacher and student in your building, whereas the other members of the team are being held accountable for the teachers they coach by *you*. That means that not only are you coaching your own teachers but you are also coaching *all* teachers via the other members of the instructional leadership team.

This is where the accountability of your team members is so crucial. Unless your school is very small, you can't coach an entire teaching staff. You have to rely on the team to do a sufficient job as instructional leaders and coaches. This is why your instructional leadership team should regularly—I would argue *daily*—meet and debrief with the primary objective being keeping you in the loop on all aspects of instructional leadership. This way if, for example, there are team members who become inundated with aspects of leadership that have little to do with instruction, it will come out in the meetings, and the team, led by you, can explore ways to ensure that instructional leadership and coaching continue to be primary functions of the team.

To What Extent Does Our Prevailing School Culture Prevent Me from Being the Instructional Leader I Need to Be?

To wrap this chapter up, this is *the* question. You can't be the instructional leader your teachers need you to be if the culture of your school doesn't support instructional leadership. Your instructional leadership team cannot be the instructional leaders you need them to be if the culture of your school doesn't support instructional leadership. Make no mistake about it: Your school—every school—has a culture. The challenge, though, is inherent in the question, Is the prevailing culture of your school conducive to high academic performance? Asked differently, Is the prevailing culture conducive to your instructional leadership team functioning optimally? You and your leadership team must be all hands on deck to lead the effort of ensuring that the culture of your school is conducive to you and your team being the instructional leaders your staff and students need you to be. Read on for more about climate and culture.

4

My Day Is Over, Now Let Me Assess It

What does instructional leadership look like for me during a typical day?

If you know my work, you know that self-reflection, which I refer to as "game film," is an integral part of all I do, beginning with my years in undergraduate school and continuing through my years as a teacher, in graduate school, as an assistant principal, as a principal, and as a speaker, consultant, and writer. The game film component of my work is a critical aspect of my productivity and success. It is equally important to who you are as an instructional leader. In fact, I will go so far as to say that you can't be optimally successful as an instructional leader if your game film is not a part of your process. Let me explain.

Game Film

For those of you who have no interest in sports, game film is simply the film of the most recent game that players and coaches watch after a game. Instead of watching it as spectators viewed it on television, they view segments of the game to learn and grow from it. They dissect and analyze it and break it down to identify what didn't work and why so that they can correct it—and to identify what worked and why to determine how to make it work even more effectively.

The study of game film is the preparation for the next game. In other words, there's no practice until the previous game's film has been reviewed. The findings of the game film review coupled with studying opponents' films are the basis for preparing for the next opponent. Now, what does game film have to do with you and your effectiveness as an instructional leader? Everything—as the discussions of self-reflection, self-assessment, self-adjustment, and self-improvement will show.

Self-Reflection

Having been a school administrator for 14 years, there is no doubt in my mind that instructional leadership is the most challenging aspect of school leadership on multiple levels, including overall effectiveness, structure, and time. You're spending a great deal of time on something that you *hope* yields the results intended and, therefore, requires a great degree of structure and organization on your part for how you plan your day. As a principal or an assistant principal, you have a lot on your plate, but the instructional aspect of your leadership requires a large chunk of your time, time that you probably don't have—particularly if the culture of your school is not conducive to you spending a lot of time on instructional leadership. In other words, if the culture of your school is working against you, being the instructional leader your school needs and requires you to be will likely be impossible.

This is where your self-reflection comes in. Unlike athletic teams, you do not need a camera and actual film. You simply need a mirror (symbolically speaking) and time. At the end of the day, when you have time to breathe, it is imperative that you carve out time to reflect on your day with intentionality, to reflect on who you were as a leader in your school. Just sit back and watch the "film," placing particular emphasis on who you were as instructional leader—if you were at all. All you are doing at this point is, nonjudgmentally, reflecting on your leadership in general and your instructional leadership in particular.

Self-Assessment

The difference between self-reflection and self-assessment is that in the self-assessment phase you will be judgmental. As I regularly tell my leadership audiences, you are not in a position to wait for your evaluator of record to inform you about your effectiveness. You need immediate feedback, and as long as you are honest with the person in your mirror, you'll get it via self-reflection. So at this juncture, you want to assess your reflection of your instructional leadership. You want to assess both who you were as instructional leader relative to the amount of time spent coaching and observing *and* who you were in each individual classroom and in each interaction with a teacher. In other words, this is an earnest, daily assessment of who you are as an instructional leader in your school. I cannot overstate the significance of this aspect of your game film because there is literally no one else who can do this for you. The assessment of your performance is on you alone. Your superiors are not going to see your every move throughout the course of a day, and they shouldn't have to. No one but you will know, which is why your assessment of yourself must be extremely detailed.

I strongly encourage you to journal your self-assessment. Keeping it in your head is not enough. It needs to be documented so that you can refer to it. It also needs to be documented so that nothing is forgotten or left out. Journaling your self-assessment boils down to good practice and serves as a bridge to self-adjustment.

A critical component of your self-assessment is whether you led instructionally at all on a given day. As a former principal, I thoroughly understand that there will be days when instructional leadership will be an impossibility. There will be days when there are so many interruptions to your formal routine that there's no possible way that you are going to be able to be the instructional leader you wish to be. This is understood. Therefore, as you engage in self-assessment, the days that you were not able to lead instructionally must be a part of your assessment of your performance as you work to determine what about your leadership led to the disruption. Was there anything about your leadership that could have prevented the interruptions? Did the situations require your presence, or could someone else have handled them? Could you have handled the situations differently, freeing up time? Were any of the situations results of aspects of your leadership that you may need to address? In other words, your assessment of yourself must be detailed to keep you on point within your overall leadership and on your quest for instructional leadership effectiveness.

Self-Adjustment

Now this step to your game film process is absolutely crucial. Self-reflection produces data. Self-assessment produces data. The question is, What are you going to do with your data? I cannot overstate the importance of using your data appropriately.

As suggested, you should journal your self-assessment. As you read through it, you should map out a plan for what comes next—your adjustment. It would be an exercise in futility to assess your instructional leadership performance, identify flaws and deficiencies, and do nothing about them. You must adjust. You must shift. You must do things differently. But the adjustment must always be rooted in the assessment.

Imagine, if you will, that you never reflect or assess and instead approach your leadership every day detached from the day prior. Your leadership would be devoid of transformative continuity. Now imagine that you engage in reflection and assessment but do nothing with the data gathered and go about your day as if the preceding day never existed. Again, your leadership would be devoid of transformative continuity. That is, the continuity is there but it's a continuity of underperformance. To become the instructional leader your school requires you to be, your leadership must be continually transformed via the relationship between your daily self-assessment and your daily self-adjustment. Ideally, the goal is to each day improve on the previous day. You must adjust according to the findings yielded by your self-assessment. You must always bring a spirit of intentionality to the adjustment phase of the process. And as with self-assessment, you should journal. Your journaling should describe in detail what that next day's adjustment will look like. It is essentially your instructional leadership plan of action for the next day.

Self-Improvement

Self-improvement is your goal as an instructional leader. To get there, you've got to self-reflect, self-assess, and self-adjust. As I stated at the outset, I feel very strongly that instructional leadership is the most challenging aspect of school leadership in terms of both quality of effectiveness and the quantity of time necessary. Instructional leadership is not easy work, but it is the most important work you will do. To that end, you must have a plan, and at the core of that plan is how you go about assessing your performance and making all of the necessary adjustments toward ongoing improvement.

The question posed at the beginning of this chapter is "What does instructional leadership look like for me during a typical day?" Said differently, "Is instructional leadership a priority of my leadership, and what is the evidence?" To that end, consider the following questions (noting that, as everyone's situation and circumstances are different, there are no universal responses to the questions).

How many teachers can I realistically coach on a given day? As I travel, many of the younger administrators will approach me and privately tell me how many classrooms they visit or teachers they coach during the course of a typical day. I usually ask them how they arrived at the number. Although the answers vary, they almost sound like quotas, particularly when they are round numbers (such as 5 or 10). I want to caution you against striving for quotas. No two days are alike. You want to assess the quantity relative to how many interactions with teachers you can have and the quality of each interaction. A daily quota is not a necessity. The necessity is to simply maximize the time that you have. You are a principal or an assistant principal. You have much on your plate, but when you have led the effort in shaping the school's culture into what you need it to be, the quantity will come, but you want it to be rooted in the quality of the interaction and not the other way around. When the goal is always quantity, quality will invariably take a back seat, and the intent of your instructional leadership and coaching will be compromised.

How do I determine which teachers need more coaching than others? There's a mantra that states, "Everything is data, and data is everything." I live by this mantra and believe it with every fiber of my being. As a leader, I was a numbers guy and tried to limit the number of decisions that were rooted in emotion. Yes, there were times—many, in fact—when decisions based on emotion had to be made, but the intent was to study the data and proceed accordingly. Which teachers need more coaching than others is both a qualitative and quantitative determination. On the qualitative side, you are observing the overall quality of the instruction in the classroom and how children are benefiting from it. On the quantitative side, you are looking at the data. What do the numbers tell you about student performance? What do the numbers tell you about multiple teachers teaching the same grade levels and same subject areas in heterogeneously grouped classrooms? This is important data to review, and the variations matter relative to why. On the qualitative side, in those classrooms where students are clearly not engaged, for example, or when classroom culture is a red flag accompanied by classroom management concerns, you know that you need to spend more time coaching those particular teachers. On the quantitative side, where the data reveal that achievement is low, for example, or there are patterns of low achievement with certain subgroups of students, you know that you need to spend more time with those particular teachers in a coaching capacity.

I cannot overstate the importance of being equitable with your teachers as a coach. Equality or equal distribution has no place in instructional leadership. When I talk about equity relative to students in the classroom, I vehemently say that equity is meeting the children where they are, as they are. Well, as it relates to instructional leadership, my line of thinking does not waver. Your teachers are not in the same place relative to their skill sets. I say you must meet the teachers where they are, as they are, and build from that point. This will help you determine which teachers need more coaching than others.

I would be remiss if I didn't point out the significance of culture as it relates to instructional leadership. In addition to everything stated, you must also focus on building a culture of instructional leadership where your presence as an instructional coach is welcomed by your staff.

What does my instructional coaching look like with any given teacher? I want you to think about what your pre-observation conferences will comprise—that is, your overall demeanor, the location of the conference (i.e., your office, a conference room, or the teacher's classroom), how you will open the meeting, how you will transition to the core of the meeting, and how you will close the meeting. Success with these conferences is not solely what you say but how you say it and where you say it.

How many classrooms can I realistically visit on a given day, and how do I determine which classrooms require more of my time than others? As I stated in the discussion on the volume of teachers seen in a day, I will say the same here regarding the volume of classrooms that you visit on any given day.

Many administrators like to launch the day with a pop-in visit of all of the classrooms in the school in the first 30 minutes or so. These visits are not to observe instruction. The purpose of these visits is just to quickly see the teacher and students in the classroom and for the teacher and the students to see you. Although they are great for contributing to a positive school culture, which has implications for the culture of the classroom, they are not going to move the academic needle. Therefore, when a leader tells me that they visit, for example, 10 or 12 classrooms a day, I have to question what this means. Does it mean that they just popped in, or does it mean that they were there for substantive periods of time? I would dare say that it would be practically impossible for a principal or an assistant principal to consistently spend substantive periods of time in 10 to 12 classrooms a day, particularly in urban or rural environments and given the number of responsibilities beyond instructional leadership. Given the number of teachers you directly supervise, if you can get into three to five classrooms in a day coupled with all of your other responsibilities, including your pre- and post-observation conferences, you have done quite well.

How quickly can I realistically provide immediate feedback to the teachers whose classrooms I visited? "Provide immediate feedback, provide immediate feedback, provide immediate feedback." We hear it all the time. It's practically cliché. But you know something? It's real. If your classroom visit is really going to matter, the timeliness of the feedback matters. Teaching is not easy. I don't care if it's an urban, rural, or suburban environment—the art of teaching, though fulfilling, is not easy. My point here, though, is that every minute of the day brings a new challenge. So much is swirling around in the mind of the teacher throughout the course of the day, including the good, the bad, and the ugly. With everything that goes on in a classroom nonstop, the teacher is not necessarily going to remember your visit of, say, two to four days prior. If your visit is going to contribute to the pedagogical growth and development of the teacher, you have got to get your feedback to the teacher as close to immediately as possible, which brings me to culture.

You must lead the effort of establishing a culture of instructional leadership and coaching within your school. This must include striving to make immediate feedback a reality and the teachers expecting it. When that culture and intentionality are absent, the process itself will probably not be taken seriously by either party and will instead just be looked at as an exercise in futility and compliance. So as you plan your weeks and structure your days, be sure to focus on getting into classrooms and building in time to discuss your thoughts and assessment of the lesson observed.

I would be remiss if I didn't remind you that, from the new teacher to the veteran teacher, your presence in the classroom has the potential of creating anxiety in the teacher. When a culture of instructional leadership is firmly entrenched in your building, the probability for anxiety decreases, but it doesn't necessarily disappear. To that end, a good habit to develop to reduce teacher anxiety is to, upon exiting the classroom, send an immediate text or email to the teacher with a short comment on something that you saw that was effective. It doesn't have to be a long note; just something to say to the teacher that some aspect of the lesson caught your attention in a good way. This way, the teacher doesn't have to spend an entire day anxious about your visit and therefore less than completely focused on the students that day. That small gesture will make a big difference.

How do I maintain a level of consistency with my instructional leadership and coaching? Two words come to mind for me with this question: *culture* and *intentionality*. Let's look at both.

- **Culture.** I have throughout said that culture is everything relative to the functioning of a school. Culture is the engine, the transmission, the steering wheel, the wheels, the heating system, the cooling system, the windshield wipers, the seats, the sound system, and so on. It's everything. If you do not have a culture for instructional leadership, you in all likelihood do not have a strong instructional leadership program. You can't just wake up in the morning and proclaim that you are going to lead instructionally if you don't have a culture in place that's conducive to instructional leadership. The culture of the school will dictate whether or not you can be the instructional leader your school needs you to be, but your leadership must dictate the culture.

- **Intentionality.** Referring to the discussion of game film, you've got to ask yourself, "Who was I today as instructional leader?" Your response matters. Instructional leadership can be taxing work, yet it is the most important aspect of your leadership. And due to the challenges and demands of the work, it is very easy, if not convenient, to say that the day, week, or month just didn't allow you to be the instructional leader you wanted to be. You must be intentional about who you need to be as an instructional leader and about what you need the culture of your school to be. To maintain a level of consistency with your instructional leadership, your commitment to leading the effort to create a culture conducive to instructional leadership coupled with your intentionality to be an effective instructional leader can never be overstated.

How am I ensuring the proficiency of my leadership team as instructional leaders? I understand that some of you reading this book are the sole administrators in your buildings. It is my hope, therefore, that you have at least one instructional coach or more on your staff, particularly one for math and one for language arts. Others of you have administrative leadership teams that comprise one or more assistant principals. As the principal, you are the leader of your school and of your leadership team. Your leadership team goes as you go. If your leadership team is going to have a collective mindset of instructional leadership and coaching, it is you who must lay the foundation and set the tone for that mindset. If you don't deem instructional leadership important, chances are that it will take a back seat with your team. If it is not a priority of your entire leadership but it is a priority of certain members of your leadership team, there is a breakdown because instructional leadership doesn't hold the same significance with each member of the team. That will translate to some teachers receiving regular coaching and others receiving compulsory once- or twice-per-year observations and evaluations—which is *not* instructional leadership. As principal, it is therefore your role and responsibility to ensure that instructional leadership is not just a "principal thing" but a "team thing." In other words, this is what we do, and we strive always to do it at a high level to be consistent with the goals, objectives, purpose, mission, and vision of our school.

How am I protecting my time while minimizing interruptions and distractions to my routine? Your time is sacred and must be protected. It must be safeguarded. Again, you have much on your plate. Your job description in and of itself is extensive, but when you consider the responsibilities that are not included in the job description, someone on the outside of this work could legitimately wonder how it is humanly possible for a principal or an assistant principal to be productive throughout a typical day. Quite frankly, I had those thoughts when I was a new administrator. I was putting in 12-plus-hour days and felt overwhelmed. But over time, I figured it out. My bottom line was how I used my time and how I protected my time. Let's explore both.

- **Using your time.** I began this chapter by talking about the significance of your game film and your ongoing planning and preparation. You must plan how you use your time and then reflect on and assess how it was *actually* used. Making adjustments to the way you use your time will be ongoing. When you earnestly examine how you use your time, you will invariably discover that there are numerous areas where your time is being grossly misused. Instructional leaders are highly effective, in part, when they become masters at using their time.

- **Protecting your time.** I saved this for the last because I have a lot to say on this topic. There's an expression that says, "Time is money." For school leaders, I will say that "Time is instructional leadership success." You cannot be the instructional leader your school requires that you be if you are not a proficient protector of your time.

Jim Rohn once said, "Time is our most valuable asset, yet we tend to waste it, kill it, and spend it rather than invest it." I couldn't agree more. Time is *everything*. As I write, it's the ninth anniversary of my heart attack, and I'm on a flight from Newark, New Jersey to Charlotte, North Carolina. Rather than sit here bopping my head to music, I am making good use of my time by writing my next book—this one. Granted, there's not a whole lot that one can do on an airplane. You are pretty much confined to a seat and, unless you're in first class, your shoulders and arms are probably touching someone you don't know. I have therefore written several books while at an altitude of 40,000 feet. I am simply making good—great, in fact—use of my time on the one hand, and I am protecting my time on the other.

As a school leader, time was an extremely valuable asset. Although I visited a great number of classrooms in my years in school leadership, those visits were not always for the purpose of formal observations. Sometimes I just wanted to stop by a classroom just to be in a classroom learning environment. When I did so, however, I would bring some work along. This way, I could be in the classroom, which was the intent, and informally observe what was happening in the room *and* get some work done (eliminating the need to do it after hours or during the school day). The bottom line is that I was making excellent use of my time. In both scenarios, I was protecting my time as opposed to wasting, killing, or spending it unwisely and consequently compromising my time. I was investing in time, which paid dividends for me—as an administrator and as an author.

As a principal or an assistant principal, there will be many days when, with piles of work to get to and get done, you wonder where the time went. Instructional leadership and coaching are on your mind, and you're wondering how you will get it done. You wind up spending additional hours in the late afternoon and evening getting caught up, and, next thing you know, you have put in 10, 12, or 14 hours. You still have to go home and do your family things, but there isn't much time for that, either, and you are worn out and want nothing more than to eat dinner and go to sleep. I keenly understand the demands on a school leader's time. It is a time-consuming position, and for that reason alone, it is not necessarily for everyone. But for me, the real questions are, how are you using your time? How are you managing your time? How are you protecting your time?

On my AP & New Principals Academy Saturday morning livestreams, I did solo sessions the entire first year. I spent five weeks on the topic of planning, organization, and time management. Each session was one hour long, and as I planned and organized each session, I discovered that there was more to discuss regarding time management than I'd previously thought. It also became clear to me that you can't talk time management without simultaneously talking planning and organization. Time is one of your most precious resources as an effective instructional leader. You can't skimp or cut corners on time. Therefore, as I planned the five-week series, I structured it around a series of 50 self-reflective questions with each session comprising 10 questions. I ask that you deeply consider the following questions for protecting your time as you strive to maximize your time as an instructional leader:

1. Is there enough time in my day to be an effective instructional leader?
2. Is 24 hours including sleep enough time for me to be productive?
3. What are my daily and weekly goals, do I have the time to meet them, and are they written?
4. What are all of the contingencies that could arise that may be preventing me from reaching my daily and weekly goals?

5. Do I have a plan for unforeseen distractions and interruptions to my planned routine?
6. How effectively do I currently manage my time?
7. How do I manage my emails?
8. Who maintains my calendar, me or my secretary?
9. Do I use a hard copy or paper calendar, or do I use an electronic calendar?
10. Who maintains my files, me or my secretary?
11. What type of filing system do I have for hard copies?
12. What type of filing system do I have for electronic documents?
13. What type of system do I have for pending documents?
14. Do I have a system for prioritizing what matters most?
15. Do I use a planner, and to what extent does it keep me organized?
16. Am I able to conceptualize and envision what my day will look like from start to finish?
17. What are some practices, routines, behaviors, and excesses that I need to purge?
18. What percentage of my day, week, month, quarter, semester, and year is devoted to my professional growth and development?
19. Do I plan my days and weeks effectively?
20. To what extent are my days thoroughly planned out through a personal daily leadership plan?
21. Do I use my time wisely?
22. Do I consider myself to be organized?
23. What level of priority do I place on being organized?
24. Am I organized to the extent that I know where I will be at all times throughout the week (as students do with a schedule)?
25. What is the evidence that I am organized?

26. Do my organizational skills allow me to get a lot done in the shortest amount of time while meeting all deadlines?
27. Do my organizational skills allow me to manage and maximize my time?
28. Have I mastered the art of maximizing my time so that there is time in the day for other activities?
29. In what ways have I helped my teachers to become organized?
30. What roles do self-reflection and self-assessment play in my overall leadership?
31. How has self-reflection made me a better manager of time?
32. What other things can I do to make better use of my time?
33. Do my organizational skills allow me to manage and maximize time?
34. Do I maintain an organized to-do list?
35. Do I have a system for developing and adhering to my to-do list?
36. Do I maintain a "powerful thoughts and ideas" list?
37. Have I written my daily and weekly goals?
38. Have I written my daily and weekly plan?
39. Does my planning consider spending time mentoring students?
40. How do I go about engaging my staff in school-level planning and decision making?
41. In what ways do data drive my planning and decision making?
42. Does my planning include after-school decompressing, following up on all unfinished work, phone calls, writing and responding to emails, debriefings, teacher

meetings, parent meetings, and meetings with members of the community?

43. Does my planning consider my own professional learning?
44. Does my planning consider how much time my body needs to recover?
45. Does my planning consider time spent with my accountability partner or thought partner?
46. Does my planning consider time spent on my exercise regimen?
47. Does my planning consider "me" time?
48. Does my planning consider family and friends time?
49. Does my planning consider my recreational time?
50. Does my planning consider self-care and self-preservation?

I give you this lengthy list of questions to say that time management as a school leader is very involved, but if you are going to get it down to a science, there are many moving parts to consider.

As you get a handle on managing your time, you must protect it. Again, your time is your most valuable asset and resource. Said differently, everything you do as a leader revolves around your use and protection of time. If you fail to effectively manage your time, your time will essentially manage you. As you get better at managing your time, remain vigilant about protecting it. Don't allow yourself to slip back to where you were or become disorganized. Protect your leadership time to preserve your instructional leadership. Compromising your leadership time could translate to ineffectiveness as a school leader, including severely compromising your intent to be the instructional leader your staff and students need you to be.

5

Someone Said, "We're Not Going to Save Them All"

Do I have a philosophy, beliefs, opinions, and ideas about how children learn based on my own research, reading, and experiences?

I f I had a dollar for every time I heard someone say, "We're not going to save them all," I wouldn't have to work another day. Though I'm exaggerating, the point is that I have heard this countless times—from educators. I call that *deficit thinking*. I never subscribed to that mentality. Of the students I've either taught or led, I have always maintained the attitude that I (we) will "save" them all and, more important, that I (we) will help them maximize their potential. As the opposite of a deficit is a surplus, I refer to the opposite of deficit thinking as *surplus thinking*—a mindset that *all* educators should possess.

All children should have a teacher with a surplus mindset every year they are in school. My definition of a *surplus-mindset teacher* is a teacher who sees greatness in every child that they encounter, even when the child doesn't see greatness in oneself or exhibit greatness in real time. A surplus-mindset teacher identifies and sees the good—the great—in every child and refuses to allow a deficit mindset to inform their thinking. A child unfortunate enough to have a deficit-mindset teacher is at an extreme disadvantage in terms of academic success, and this is where you as instructional leader come in. A child can conceivably spend a year or more with a deficit-mindset teacher if that teacher is never monitored or had the mindset coached out of them. If you live (lead) a reality where visiting classrooms is not a part of your daily routine, I can assure you that the probability that many children will suffer is high. Marinate in that for a minute.

When You Walk into a Classroom to Observe, Who Are You?

I divided this chapter into two sections, the first of which comprises the following questions:

- Am I a fan or a spectator in the classroom?
- Do I understand that the zip codes (of students, teachers, and administrators) matter?
- Do I understand that home learning experiences and the home learning environment matter?

Let's look at each.

Am I a Fan or a Spectator in the Classroom?

You may have looked at this question and asked yourself, "What is Principal Kafele talking about?" Consider this scenario:

A woman is given two tickets to a professional football game. An athlete all her life, though she loves sports generally, football is her thing. She knows the sport so well that she can hold her own in a conversation on the game with experts. She is conversant in every aspect of the game and knows its history. Her best friend attends the game with her even though she dislikes sports, including football, as she feels obliged because they're close friends.

Once they are at the game, the woman who is a huge fan of football thoroughly enjoys it. She knows and understands everything that's happening on the offensive side of the field as well as what's happening on the defensive side. She's quite vocal and expresses a variety of emotions as she repeatedly yells at the players during certain plays. *She is a true "fan" of the sport.*

Meanwhile, her friend is enjoying her time at the game with her. What's most important to her is enjoying time with her friend. The game is of no interest to her; she doesn't know, like, or understand it. What matters to her is spending a day with her best friend and watching her friend's excitement. *She is nothing more than a "spectator" who has no interest in what's happening on the field.*

You may still be asking yourself, "Where is Principal Kafele going with this?" That one woman is a *fan* and the other a *spectator* is key to where I am going. Consider this scenario:

As part of a morning walkthrough at an elementary school, two administrators visit the classroom of a first-year teacher in her first month of teaching. The intent is to have two sets of eyes on the lesson they will observe. They enter a 2nd grade general education classroom, sit on opposite sides of the room, and observe the lesson. Both administrators are assistant principals, and I'll refer to them as Assistant Principal A and Assistant Principal B. Assistant Principal A, a former high school mathematics teacher and a brand-new AP in his first month, is the evaluator of record of the teacher being observed. Assistant Principal B, a former 3rd grade teacher, is in her fourth year as an assistant principal.

As the APs observe the lesson, Assistant Principal A is thinking, "This is a great lesson. The teacher is in full control and clearly commands the room. The children are sitting very quietly and appear to be focused. As the teacher delivers instruction, four or five students consistently raise their hands to answer questions, which is not bad so early in the school year. The students fully comply with the rules posted on the wall. I am pleased with and impressed by what I see in this classroom."

On the other side of the room, Assistant Principal B is observing the lesson and thinking, "This classroom is extremely teacher-driven, teacher-directed, teacher-centered, and teacher-dominant. The children, except for the four or five students of 21 students on the roster who consistently raise their hands to answer questions, are disengaged. The children are sitting in rows and are not given the opportunity to engage with one another or participate in their own learning. The lesson doesn't take into consideration the academic individuality of the students. Instead, it treats the students as if they all learn in the same way. The teacher is very strong-willed, and the children seem somewhat intimidated by her. So many missed opportunities for student success in this environment. The amount of coaching needed to help this teacher to develop is immense but definitely doable. At this juncture, however, I have a ton of work to do in a short period of time to help this teacher develop pedagogically."

Two administrators observing the same lesson have dramatically different takeaways. The variables that stand out are the backgrounds and experiences of the administrators and the inexperience of the teacher. Clearly, the mode of instruction for a classroom of 2nd graders is not conducive to engaging them throughout the course of a lesson, day, week, month, or school year.

Referring to my example of a fan and a spectator, Assistant Principal A is operating as a "spectator" in this instance. Although I won't go so far as to call him a spectator in the classroom, I will say that as one new to school leadership and elementary education, he has much to learn and understand about the dynamics of teaching and learning in a 2nd grade classroom. He doesn't yet know the "game" because in watching it, it's clear that he doesn't really know and understand what 2nd grade elementary instruction should look like.

Assistant Principal B, on the other hand, is clearly a "fan" in this instance, as evidenced by her takeaways. She is in a better position than Assistant Principal A to effectively coach the teacher instructionally. She can also assist in coaching Assistant Principal A, which speaks volumes about the role of the members of a school's leadership team.

Let's expand on this scenario. First look at Assistant Principal A and imagine a school where the leadership team seldom, if ever, meets to talk about instruction and the principal seldom, if ever, meets with assistant principals to talk about instruction. There's an expression that says, "You don't know what you don't know." If Assistant Principal A doesn't surround himself with colleagues, professionals, and experts who *do* know, or professional learning that counters who he is in real time and will help him grow, who he is currently could have long-term consequences for the children of the teachers he supervises. As, as it stands, there's nothing in place to allow this new leader to grow instructionally. A long stretch of his leadership could be spent operating as nothing more than a mere spectator continually impressed by mediocrity.

Let's now revisit the opening question of this chapter: *Do I have a philosophy, beliefs, opinions, and ideas about how children learn based on my own research, reading, and experiences?* This question is asking you who you are when you walk into a classroom to observe instruction. Are you walking in as an empty vessel, easily impressed by what *appears* on the surface to be satisfactory, or do you walk into classrooms with particular expectations given what you know about teaching, learning, and the students in your school? Your answer matters. In other words, when you walk into a classroom to observe instruction, are you Assistant Principal A or Assistant Principal B?

Do I Understand That the Zip Codes (of Students, Teachers, and Administrators) Matter?

As a school leader and instructional leader, you must acknowledge that the zip codes of your students absolutely matter. Schools comprise children of different races, cultures, ethnicities, and historical backgrounds, and in far too many instances, those differences determine their zip codes and their life experiences, realities, challenges, obstacles, needs, interests, pressures, demands, goals, aspirations, and opportunities. The realities and available opportunities of children in various racial, ethnic, and cultural groups in schools are a consequence of the groups to which they belong. Therefore, no teacher is in a position to say that they do not see the race, ethnicity, or culture of children. In other words, color or culture blindness has no place in the classroom. The racial, ethnic, and cultural differences of children must be acknowledged, appreciated, accentuated, understood, and celebrated.

The teachers you supervise are first and foremost teachers of children, not of content. They happen to teach the children content. The children in your school cannot afford to have teachers who prioritize content over children. One can know their content inside and out, but if one doesn't know children, the content knowledge may be for naught because of the lack of understanding of how to transfer the content to the minds of the children, including children who may not "look like the teacher." How are you going to effectively teach a child who you do not really know and understand racially, ethnically, culturally, or historically? Children are not just children. They are individuals with vastly different life experiences, and large swaths of children have life experiences that are rooted in the marginalization of Black, Brown, and other underserved people. Your teachers must have the knowledge and skill set to be able to meet the academic, social, and emotional needs of each of your students, which can be particularly challenging if they are unfamiliar with life in the zip codes of the children they teach.

As an instructional leader, this is an important component of your overall leadership and coaching of the teachers you supervise. Your teachers must be culturally competent, particularly when working with children whose backgrounds differ from theirs. Are you conversant in this type of discussion? Are you comfortable with this type of discussion? Do you have the background, expertise, and cultural competence needed to engage your teachers in this type of discussion? Are you able to have this discussion devoid of stereotypes and generalizations? Does your zip code limit your ability to effectively engage in this type of discussion? As uncomfortable as such a discussion may be (and as uncomfortable as this portion of this book may make you), it is a necessary aspect of instructional leadership if your historically marginalized students are going to have a fighting chance at success within and outside the school building.

Do I Understand That Home Learning Experiences and the Home Learning Environment Matter?

Expanding on the previous section, your teachers must understand that the experiential backgrounds of their students will dictate readiness to learn—particularly readiness to learn how to read and to compute. If your student population includes historically underserved groups, that can never be ignored or dismissed. The youngster who arrives at school where all of his economic needs are being met has a higher level of readiness to learn than the child who goes to bed hungry every night or arrives at school hungry every morning. The youngster who arrives at school where all of his emotional needs are being met has a higher level of readiness than the child whose experiences at home have traumatized her. Such situations have implications for a child's academic performance and the teacher's pedagogical effectiveness.

Picture a child whose home environment is so challenging that he's never been read to or is so traumatic that focusing on your teachers' lessons is virtually impossible. Do your teachers understand this? Do you understand this? Are scenarios such as these part of the dialogue between you and your teachers? Consider the implications for children when such dialogue is absent from the discussion.

Amid all of this is you—an instructional leader in your school. Imagine that everything stated above is your reality but your leadership reality is one that prevents you from being a fixture in classrooms as an instructional leader. The self-reflective question then becomes "What is it about my leadership that benefits my teachers instructionally and academically?" Said differently, "What is my value instructionally to the teachers I supervise?" It is my strong contention that we can not only save them all but also position ourselves to help them maximize their potential. As an instructional leader, you must believe this.

Instructional Leadership and Equity

In this section, I want to briefly discuss equity as it relates to your instructional leadership. Before I get started, however, I want to be fully transparent about the word *equity*. I consider equity one of the most important, if not *the* most important, words in education, particularly for historically marginalized populations of people and children. I spent weeks wrestling with whether to include this section. Politically, the word *equity* has become so controversial that I didn't want to risk having this important work maligned because of one section of this book. But I rationalized that I stand behind equity. As it's at the core of my educational existence, I can't run away from it to avoid the politics surrounding it. I believe so strongly in classrooms where equitable practices yield equitable opportunities for children that avoiding this discussion would have meant that my authentic self wouldn't have been in the pages of this book, and as that mattered to me, I included this section.

There are a ton of equity practitioners, scholars, researchers, presenters, and authors out there doing phenomenal work. I try to keep up with all of them. In this context, the challenge for the readers and listeners of this vast work is that there isn't a universal definition for equity. It varies, which forces the reader or listener to determine which information is most applicable to them. As a lifelong equitable practitioner long before "equity" became a part of the education lexicon, I engaged in a practice for which I didn't have a name. I was highly intentional about meeting children where they were, as they were. I understood the differences that I referenced in the previous section, and when I say differences, I mean differences inclusive of and beyond race, ethnicity, and culture. My classrooms and school were predominantly Black, but the differences between students extended beyond race, ethnicity, and culture, and as their teacher, assistant principal, and principal, I always took that into consideration.

When equity started to explode as a formal practice around 2012, I was at last able to give a name to what I'd been doing, and my definition of equity became this:

Meeting young people where they are . . . *as they are!*

To this day, in the equity space, this definition defines my work. I really do not see how instructional leaders can avoid this definition, regardless of the racial, ethnic, or cultural composition of your school. My premise is that if children are to have a chance to maximize their potential during their school years, they must have teachers who are willing and have the wherewithal to "meet them where they are . . . as they are." As instructional leader, is meeting young people where they are, as they are, a part of your coaching? Is meeting young people where they are, as they are, a part of what you are looking for when observing instruction? Is meeting young people where they are, as they are, who you are as an instructional leader? For further insight around my thoughts on equity, please refer to my book *The Equity & Social Justice Education 50* (2021).

I literally preach, "Meeting young people where they are . . . as they are" all over the United States and abroad throughout the year, every year. It is one of my mantras. But I argue that it can't be spoken or practiced in isolation. It is my strong contention that the following questions must be addressed regularly by the teacher to meet young people where they are, as they are:

- **Do I *know* where they are (awareness)?** Your teachers must *know* where students are academically, socially, and emotionally, which must drive a part of your coaching as an instructional leader.
- **Do I have *reason to know* where they are (curiosity)?** Your teachers must feel that their students' academic, social, and emotional growth and development warrant knowing them where they are, as they are. They won't be able to meet them where they are, as they are, if they're not genuinely curious, which must drive a part of your coaching as an instructional leader.
- **Do I *desire* to know where they are (compassion)?** Your teachers must have a desire to know where their students are academically, socially, and emotionally. On the emotional side, this is the requisite relationship building that must occur. You can't meet them where they are if there's no desire, determination, or urge to know where they are. This must drive a part of your coaching as an instructional leader.
- **Do I *understand* where they are (grasp)?** This is a big one. While the first question states, "Do I *know* where they are?" this question goes deeper and asks whether you *understand* where they are. In other words, are you aware

of the layers of a given youngster's reality? Do you understand the youngster beyond simply knowing him? For example, you can *know* that a youngster is living in abject poverty inclusive of the concomitant challenges. While knowing this matters, the real question is, Do you *understand* it? Do you understand the complexities of living in poverty? Empathy is derived from your understanding, not simply your knowledge. This, too, must drive a part of your coaching as an instructional leader.

- Do I *know how* to meet them where they are (application)? Lastly, in the application phase, do your teachers know how to meet their students where they are? I cannot overstate your role as instructional leader in assisting your teachers with the application process. You can't meet your students where they are if you don't know *how* to meet them where they are. Although theory has its place, your teachers must be proficient in the application phase. This, too, must drive a part of your coaching as an instructional leader.

A Final Thought on Equity and You as Instructional Leader

If your students are to have an equitable chance for success, it is imperative that they be taught by an equity-mindset teacher. That is, a teacher who uses a variety of developmentally appropriate instructional strategies that consider the differing academic, social, and emotional needs of *each* of the learners in a student-centered, culturally responsive, culturally relevant, barrier-free, equity-mindset classroom where student individuality, student racial/cultural identity, and student voice matter exponentially.

My ASCD book *The Equity & Social Justice Education 50* (2021) comprises a lot of what the foregoing definition entails. As an instructional leader advocating for each student in your school, it is your responsibility to make sure that your advocacy via instructional leadership and coaching ensures that the teachers you supervise make it a rule to meet students where they are, as they are.

6

Visiting Classrooms
Is Not Enough

***What is the significance of the pre- and post-
observation conversation, including the analysis
of data, to my leadership instructionally?***

lthough getting into classrooms is good and getting into
classrooms for long periods of time is better, attaching
those visits to pre-observation and post-observation conversations is best.

Popping into classrooms but doing nothing with the information gathered doesn't benefit teachers. It simply means that
you were there. By the same token, popping into classrooms
without an associated game plan, intended outcome, or strategy
again means that you were simply there, and it translates to . . .
nothing relative to the pedagogical growth and development of
the teachers. Who you are as a coach matters. If coaching is not
occurring, you are sending your teachers into the game without coaching them from the sidelines. Instructional leadership
and coaching comprise the pre-observation conversation, the
observation, and the post-observation conversation. Let's take
a look at each.

The Pre-Observation Conversation

The pre-observation conversation, what is typically referred to as the pre-observation conference, is a critical component of your leadership in general and your instructional leadership in particular. I refer to it as a conversation to take the sting out of the process and to the extent possible make teachers feel at ease.

The pre-observation conversation is rooted in the self-reflective question "What is my purpose for observing this lesson?" The purpose should be detailed in the conversation with the teacher. I will now ask that you hold up your mirror and ask yourself the following self-reflective questions, which stem from the opening chapter question:

- Do I deem the pre-observation conversation significant to the professional growth and development of my teachers?
- How intentional am I about meeting with my teachers prior to visiting their classrooms, and what is the evidence?
- Do I routinely meet with individual teachers regarding instruction?
- How many teachers do I meet with on a given day, and why?
- What is the ratio of the number of times I visit classrooms and the number of times I meet with teachers before visiting their classrooms?
- What is my area of focus during the conversations?
- Do the conversations target specific skill areas and practices?
- Am I conversant in the skill areas and practices discussed?
- Am I comfortable engaging teachers in these conversations?
- Are the individual teachers comfortable engaging in these conversations with me?

- How do I ensure that teachers welcome these conversations?
- How do I ensure that teachers feel at ease during these conversations?
- How do I ensure that teachers contribute to these conversations?
- How do I approach teachers who may resist coaching?
- How do I initiate conversations about areas that I feel need improvement without creating tension?
- How do I limit distractions when meeting with teachers about instruction?
- How do I maximize my time in these instructional conversations with teachers while minimizing the amount of time that the meetings take?
- Do I listen attentively to the teachers and not interrupt them?
- Do the conversations that I have with my teachers positively affect their instructional practices?
- How do I determine which teachers require more coaching than others?
- Are there any teachers who I feel don't require coaching, and if so, why?
- Do I inform the teachers when I will visit their classroom, or do I show up randomly and unannounced?
- What role does data analysis play in my conversations with teachers?
- Do the teachers I supervise use data to inform their instructional practices?
- In what other ways do the teachers I supervise use the data that relate to their students?
- Is the analysis of data on aspects other than discipline a priority for my assistant principals?

- What do the data tell me (as instructional leader) about the academic needs of my school?
- What do the data tell me (as instructional leader) about the pedagogical and performance needs of my teachers?
- What do the data tell me (as instructional leader) about the academic needs of individual students?
- Do I consider the data on the teachers I supervise a reflection of who I am as an instructional leader?
- In what ways do my district's evaluation rubric and instrument align with my coaching?

While I was tempted to elaborate on the questions, I quickly concluded that I could write a chapter on each one. So I instead encourage you to think deeply about each question relative to your role as instructional leader and consider how it applies to who you are, are not, and wish to be as instructional leader.

I will tell you that it's always best to visit the classrooms of your teachers before your initial conversations with them. If you haven't seen the teachers in action, there's no real basis for the conversation in terms of identifying areas to develop. At the beginning of the school year, give your teachers an opportunity to get to know their students and occasionally pop into classrooms. You may want to spend more time in their classrooms in the second or third week to identify strengths and weaknesses that will serve as the basis for the conversations.

The underlying self-reflective question relative to the entire process is "What is my purpose for observing this lesson?" Although on the surface it seems like a commonsense question, it can be a very complex question because there is so much to see in a classroom. You are a school administrator, which means that your duties and responsibilities are endless. You do not have the time to enter a classroom and observe it randomly or mindlessly. Just as writing an essay, a blog post, a research paper, a dissertation, or a book requires a particular focus, entering a classroom in your capacity as instructional leader requires a particular focus. It will be rooted in the pre-observation conversations where you and the teacher can mutually agree on areas to collaborate to strengthen the teacher's skill sets. It answers the question "What is my purpose for observing this lesson?"

Now imagine you are not one to engage in pre-observation conversations and instead just pop into classrooms and observe instruction without an area of focus that the teacher is aware of. Will the basis of your visit be to take in everything the eyes can see? Will it benefit the teacher? Probably not. That would be a colossal waste of your time. The whole process of developing a teacher is, and must be, methodical. This doesn't mean that you will be wearing blinders and won't be able to see anything else in the classroom. No. You will see the entire classroom and may want to make note of some things for subsequent conversations, but your real-time focus will be what you discussed during the pre-observation conversation.

Before moving on to the observation, I must say this: Instructional coaching is a methodical process. It's a "grow ya," not a "gotcha," and it is another reason why I choose *conversation* over *discussion*. I want teachers to feel that they are an integral part of the process. To that end, as you are in the growth and development stage, avoid popping into classrooms unannounced. Set a date and time for a classroom visit, do everything in your power to ensure you are there and on time, and observe everything that was discussed. Later in the process, as the teacher is growing within the area of focus, you can pop in unannounced. For now, the focus is developing a teacher in a particular area, and you want to be methodical throughout the process. At the conclusion of the observation, provide feedback and follow up as soon as possible.

The Observation

As you are starting this process with the teacher at the beginning of a new school year, it is crucial that you refrain from cold calls or showing up unannounced. As I stated, it's about growing teachers, not catching them out, and the process is methodical. You want to be able to have the conversation and then observe what you discussed unfold in the classroom during instruction. You mustn't allow yourself to feel that the teacher will put on a performance if they know you're coming. You want the teacher to know you are coming so that you can observe everything that was discussed, which provides you with good data to discuss during the post-observation conversation. You are at once intentionally establishing, building, and nurturing a culture of instructional leadership where the teacher welcomes your input toward the pedagogical growth and development that will make them a more effective teacher.

To be clear, there is nothing summative about these observations. They're all formative. You and the teacher are developing ... the teacher. This process is not solely about you; it's about the collegiality of you and the teacher and, by extension, the academic growth and development of the students. The observations are summative when they are tied to a formal evaluation.

You undoubtedly learned how to script a lesson, a vital skill, in grad school. You want to write down all pertinent aspects of the lesson as opposed to relying on your memory—a habit I had to break. I had to train myself to be copious in my scripting of the lesson. I would later organize my notes so that I could have as comprehensive a follow-up conversation as possible, and I strongly encourage you to do the same. Going into a post-observation conversation unprepared to discuss the fullness of the lesson observed defeats the entire purpose.

I will also say that you may not need an entire block or period to observe everything that you need to. Again, the process is methodical, and you have a busy schedule. As these observations are not summative, there's room for flexibility. Focus solely on what you need to see, rooted in the conversation you had with the teacher prior to the observation.

After the observation, despite the teacher's comfort with the process, there's a chance that your visit will cause the teacher anxiety. In the age of sending text and email messages on smartphones, a great practice would be to immediately send the teacher a text or an email message about something good that you observed to allay any anxiety the teacher may have about your visit. The last thing you want is the teacher spending the rest of the day anxious about your visit as opposed to concentrating on the students in front of them.

Lastly, your district's evaluation rubric and instrument can never be detached from this process because both are the standard by which the teacher will be evaluated. Both must align with your coaching.

The Post-Observation Conversation

This—the feedback—is a critical component of the process. It's cliché to say that "follow-up feedback must be immediate." The truth of the matter is that this cliché hasn't lost its relevance. The feedback has to be immediate because you don't want the details of what was observed to get lost over time. If you meet with the teacher on the lesson you observed days after having done so, the teacher will have taught several lessons after being observed and may not accurately recall what's written in your notes. So it's imperative that the period of time between the observation and your post-observation conversation be very short.

In the conversation, you'll want to review all that was discussed in the pre-observation conversation to set the tone for the conversation around the lesson you observed. Remember that you were in the classroom to observe what was discussed, not to take in and analyze everything the eyes could see. The things that fall outside the realm of the conversation can be conveyed as a compliment on something that worked well, red flags, and everything in between. The focus of the conversation must be what was observed, with a particular emphasis on strategies for improving areas of deficiency.

I think it is worth repeating here the significance of the word *conversation*. This meeting, coupled with the pre-observation conversation, can never be one-sided with you lecturing. For the teacher to embrace the entire concept, it has to be a conversation.

After your meetings, I want you to regularly ask yourself the following self-reflective questions:

- How much time elapsed between my observation of the lesson and my follow-up or post-observation conversation?
- If more than a day elapsed, did it adversely affect the quality of the conversation?
- How substantive was the feedback that I provided?
- Was my feedback on the lesson well received by the teacher?
- How did I handle the teacher's objections or disagreements?
- Did my observation of the lesson capture the essence of what was discussed in the pre-observation conversation?
- Did I engage the teacher in the conversation, or did I do all of the talking?
- After reviewing my notes and reflecting on the lesson, did I compile solutions or strategies for success before the conversation?
- Was the teacher at ease during the conversation?

- Was I at ease during the conversation?
- Did I listen attentively to the teacher during the conversation?
- Does the teacher understand that there was nothing summative about the observation or the follow-up conversation?

These questions are as critical to you becoming a proficient instructional coach as the pre-observation questions.

Ongoing Coaching

In a school where the leadership only pops into classrooms for substantive periods of time during evaluation season and evaluations occur one to three times per year, nothing in this book is relevant to your practice. And if you are in a low-performing school, your students are suffering tremendously in large part because the concepts detailed in this book are not an inherent part of your leadership.

Although school leadership encompasses much more than instructional leadership, instructional leadership should be at your core as a school leader. You must be intentional about how you incorporate instructional leadership into your daily routine. I do not want to give the impression that you should dedicate your entire day to instructional leadership. My intent is to encourage you to position instructional leadership so that it becomes your priority within your overall leadership. As I stated previously, every teacher you supervise does not need the same thing from you, and you shouldn't approach them in the same way. "Equality" has no place in instructional leadership. It is all about being "equitable" in your collegial relationships with your teachers based on their pedagogical needs. Use your limited time wisely. Treating all of your teachers the same is counterproductive.

Culture Matters

I cannot overstate the importance of culture. Instructional leadership and coaching cannot operate in a vacuum. For instructional leadership to work as intended, there must be in place a schoolwide culture that all embrace and that translates to "This is who we are." If you and your team are not intentional about establishing a culture of instructional leadership, it will probably never be fully embraced by those for whom it was created—your teachers.

Creating a culture of instructional leadership requires ongoing discussions with your staff in staff meetings, PLCs, and so on so that they understand that your classroom visits are not summative or invasions of teachers' classrooms but rather designed to ensure that everyone is striving for excellence—and instructional excellence is one of the many ways to achieve it.

7

There Must Be More to Me Now Than Who I Was Then

What do I know about excellent pedagogy beyond who I was as a classroom teacher?

This particular question really resonates with me. To give you context, I became a school administrator in 1998. A public speaker since 1986, I began speaking to teachers and school administrators in 2004 but didn't leave the principalship until 2011. What I discovered early on when speaking to teachers and administrators was that I was sharing in my presentations much of what I did as a teacher and administrator with the expectation that what worked for me would work for them. Although I've never been challenged on that notion, the wisdom that comes with experience kicked in, and it occurred to me that I was presenting as if my audiences would become versions of me. All I knew relative to my presentations was what I had already done. For a while, I thought that was fine. However, I came to realize that it wasn't OK.

Much of who I was in the classroom and as a leader was rooted in who I was as an individual. Principal Kafele was informed by Baruti K. Kafele. I therefore concluded that I couldn't expect everyone in my audiences to embrace all I was saying and infuse it into their practices. Although my advice may have theoretically been sound, it may not have necessarily aligned with who the audience members were personally.

In my early days as a speaker, I implored principals to deliver powerful morning messages to their schools each day to lay a solid foundation for learning and set the tone for overall expectations. I didn't consider that everyone isn't wired to grab a microphone and deliver a powerful message. I discovered that I needed to rethink what the morning message may comprise and what it might sound like so that every administrator in the room could identify with and relate to what I intended the morning message to be. I never veered from the belief that the principal should deliver the morning message (not to be confused with the student-led morning announcements). However, I no longer give the impression that the message had to be as energetic as mine was. I now contend that the principal must be who they are while also always striving to earn the trust and respect of the students, so that they never have to pretend to be someone else to capture students' attention.

At the end of my fourth year as a classroom teacher, I was named the school, district, county, and New Jersey State finalist for Teacher of the Year. As a result, in my mind, I knew something about great teaching. In hindsight, however, what I knew was great teaching that worked for "Mr. Kafele the teacher." All I knew at the time was what worked for me in my classroom. When I became an administrator soon after, everything I said and modeled relative to my limited experience as an instructional leader was rooted in Mr. Kafele the teacher. If I was going to become the instructional leader my staff needed me to be, I needed to know more than who I was as a classroom teacher. I needed to know pedagogy. If I was going to become an effective instructional leader, my knowledge base had to extend further than who Mr. Kafele was.

What about you? What do you know about excellent pedagogy beyond who you were as a teacher? As the chapter title states, there must be more to you now than who you were then as a classroom teacher. Our personal successes in the classroom yesterday may not have fully qualified us to be proficient instructional leaders today. We must continually be intentional in adding value to the teachers we supervise instructionally through our ongoing professional growth and development regarding great pedagogy.

I will now go deeper into this discussion via the self-reflection questions that follow.

What Sort of Professional Learning Am I Ensuring That My Teachers Are Receiving Relative to Their Pedagogy *for the Students We Serve?*

I will begin by reflecting on inservice days back when I was a teacher and a principal. Because of the number of days that school is required to be in session, inservice days were minimal—three or four half-days (1 p.m. to 4 p.m.) at most. This meant that at the building level, the best we could offer our teachers relative to inservice time was 9 to 12 hours of professional learning per school year, which was grossly insufficient and inadequate. The good thing, however, was that there were breakout sessions, and between the building-level administrators and the central office administrators, we were able to connect teachers to sessions that met most of their classroom needs (as opposed to everyone attending the same session regardless of need).

There's a hat that accompanies your instructional leadership hat—your professional developer hat. It goes hand in glove with who you are as an instructional leader. You really can't be one without being the other. In other words, at the building level, you can't consider yourself a true instructional leader if professional developer is not a part of your repertoire and vice versa.

As an instructional leader, your instructional coaching is professional development and professional learning for the teachers you supervise. The question then is, What is your level of involvement in other aspects of professional learning for your teachers? As the principal or an assistant principal in your school, this aspect of your leadership can never be overlooked.

What Experts Are We Bringing In?

Quality matters. When you have the luxury of bringing in presenters and consultants, you want to vet them properly. What are the specific needs of and challenges and obstacles faced by your school? What are the specific needs of and challenges and obstacles faced by your teachers? What are the specific needs of and challenges and obstacles faced by your students? The needs may be academic, social, emotional, and so forth. You want to consider all of the needs, challenges, and obstacles that affect learning in the classroom because a presenter, no matter how engaging, motivating, and empowering, is not always enough.

Does the presenter possess the technical knowledge to move your academic needle? Does the presenter have experience working with students and staff with comparable needs and who face challenges and obstacles comparable to those of your students and staff? If you are an urban school, does the presenter have experience working with teachers who teach in urban environments? Does the presenter have a track record of success in environments comparable to yours? It doesn't matter how phenomenal a teacher you were if your strengths are not transferable to each of the teachers you supervise. You need to bring in people with expertise in areas in which you are not expert.

The sources of professional learning that I presented in the Introduction—conferences, institutes, academies, seminars, lectures, presentations, podcasts, livestreams, videos, modules, books, journals, blogs, professional learning networks/social media—are not intended to replace your value as an instructional leader because the authors, presenters, hosts, and so on will not be providing teachers with feedback on the implementation. That can only happen at the building or central office level via you and your leadership team, instructional coaches, and central office supervisors and directors. The aforementioned sources of professional learning can supplement your efforts. There are a lot of professional learning resources out there, and as an instructional leader, you should be tapping into all of them.

Does the Pedagogy in My Classrooms Ensure That Cultural Relevance in Instruction Is Normalized?

In staying consistent with the theme of this chapter, let's say that you were superb as a classroom teacher in an environment where the students were White and the curriculum was Eurocentric across content areas where Eurocentrism is central. That would translate to students being exposed to curriculum and instruction to which, on the basis of race, they could relate and identify with as they are White. In this hypothetical scenario, learning was culturally relevant for them as it spoke to who they were racially. In a different scenario, you are the teacher of a racially diverse classroom and the curriculum is, again, Eurocentric. Because you understand your role in a racially diverse classroom, you understand the importance of ensuring that instruction is relatable and identifiable to *every* learner.

As an instructional leader in your school, it is important that your conversations with your teachers include strategies that ensure that teaching and learning are culturally relevant and that the relationships between teachers and students are culturally responsive.

Does the Pedagogy in My Classrooms Ensure That Equity Is Normalized?

Expanding on the previous hypothetical, let's say that you were the teacher in a classroom where the students were taught and treated equally (i.e., the same) in a school that lacked racial diversity, and you were successful. But now, you are in a school replete with racial, cultural, and socioeconomic diversity where the learning environment differs greatly. In a situation such as that, equity must be the norm because of the diversity in the school and classrooms.

Do you know what an equitable classroom learning environment entails? Are you knowledgeable enough about equity to be able to help the teachers you supervise develop equitable learning environments? Does every child taught by the teachers you supervise have equitable opportunities for success? Is equity on a path of normalization in your school? Do you still have questions about what equity is and what it isn't? To me, "meeting young people where they are, as they are" is a necessary component of great classroom teaching.

What Sort of PD Relative to My Development as an Instructional Leader or Coach Am I Being Exposed To?

The bottom line is that you are no longer a teacher. You are a school administrator. However, you are not the stereotypical school administrator who walks around the school keeping order. No. Your role relative to instruction is just as significant as the classroom teacher's but in a very different way. While the teacher teaches the lesson, your role while wearing your instructional leader/professional developer hat is, in a nutshell, to ensure that teaching and learning are happening at high levels via superior instructional leadership and support.

I'm in no way asserting that, given your role as principal or assistant principal and everything you have on your plate, you will devote your entire day to instructional leadership; that would not be practical. What I'm saying is that who you are in your instructional leadership capacity must be at the core of your overall leadership. The reason that your students walk into your school every day is to learn. Everything else is a vehicle to get there and to enhance and broaden learning. The reason that your teachers walk into your school every day is to teach. Your role, then, is to facilitate the entire process. If you are daily bombarded with things other than instruction and learning (e.g., administrative duties, operational duties, discipline), you can't be the instructional leader your school needs you to be. It simply won't be possible.

To that end, what sort of professional learning that helps you to become a better instructional leader are you exposing yourself to? What sort of professional learning that allows you to be better organized with the structure of your day and time as a school leader are you exposing yourself to? What sort of professional learning that enhances your professional coaching with how you go about engaging your teachers in your pre- and post-observation conversations are you exposing yourself to? What professionals who have already figured out much of what you are trying to accomplish around instructional leadership and coaching are you engaging with?

Admittedly, instructional leadership is not easy work. The process itself is very complex, and creating the time and space for it can be challenging. As I reflect on my years as a school administrator, I can think of nothing outside of school safety that ate away at me more than instructional leadership. So if it's professional learning or just surrounding yourself with the right thought partner or accountability partner, make your growth and development as an instructional leader an ongoing priority.

8

Maximizing Your Administrative Leadership Team

What is the role of my administrative leadership team in establishing a culture of instructional leadership?

Discipline, discipline, discipline. Everywhere I go I see administrators—assistant principals, in particular—handling discipline. Although I get that someone's got to do it, I've regularly preached all over the country that the problem is not the children, their parents, their neighborhoods, or their economic conditions. While societal challenges affect us all, particularly children, they don't have to dominate our schools.

I recently attended a Broadway play in New York City, at a theater in the middle of Times Square. Although a *lot* goes on in Times Square, the vibe of Times Square was not felt in the theater before, during, or after the play. Why? Because there is a culture in the theater that dictates the conduct of theatergoers.

Not far from Broadway is Madison Square Garden, where I recently attended a basketball game. The crowd and the atmosphere, both electric, were dramatically different from that in the Broadway theater. Why? Because there is a culture in the arena that dictates the conduct of fans.

Lastly, in my younger years, I spoke in various juvenile detention centers. Upon arrival, the wardens would tell me about why the young men to whom I would be speaking were in the facilities, warning me that their educational backgrounds and attention spans were short. The wardens in every facility would advise me to speak for no more than 10 or 15 minutes, as they felt I would lose the attention of the young men if I spoke longer. I would typically speak for 60 to 90 minutes—and the young men were completely engaged the entire time. The puzzled expressions on the faces of wardens let me know that wasn't the norm. The young men gave me their full attention throughout the presentation. Why? Lean in and hear me well on this one: Because I created a culture within that environment that dictated the conduct of the young men. That is, I had to immediately and on the spot replace the established culture with a new one. I had to learn and ultimately understand the environment in which I was presenting prior to my presentation so that I could open with words and exhibit a demeanor that would instantly capture the attention of those young men. Had I spoken to them within the culture that prevailed, they likely would not have heard me or received my message.

My point is that culture works the same way in the schools that you lead. Again, it's not the children, the parents, the neighborhoods, or the economic conditions—all of which are significant and none of which should be ignored. However, your school does not have to be a reflection of those challenges and conditions. Undesirable student behaviors are typically a reflection of your school's current culture, which may be counterproductive. Chances are good that when administration spends inordinate amounts of time addressing discipline, those undesirable behaviors are a direct response to the prevailing culture of the building. It is the influence—not the *control* but the *influence*—of the leadership that launches the schoolwide effort toward cultural transformation. When the culture shifts, student behaviors, staff behaviors, and expectations also shift, and the time that administrators need to spend disciplining children decreases.

Remember: The children are in school to learn. *You being inundated with discipline will not raise the math and reading scores.* If learning is going to occur at a high level and assessment scores are going to soar, there must be a culture in place that is conducive to this vision becoming your reality. Assistant principals in particular cannot be reduced to full-time (or majority-of-the-time) disciplinarians. In schools where they are, what is required is a dramatic shift from the prevailing culture to a culture of academic excellence with instructional leadership at the core. Your administrative leadership team (ALT), a subset of the larger leadership team that typically comprises both administrative and nonadministrative leaders, must lead the effort in establishing a culture of instructional leadership—the anchor and a bridge to a culture of academic excellence.

The focus for this chapter is the important role of the ALT in leading the effort of establishing and building a culture of instructional leadership. For the purposes of this book, I cannot overstate the importance of the ALT to a school on so many levels in general and instructionally in particular. It is for that reason that this chapter is by far the longest in the book.

As I've stated throughout this book, your priorities within your administrative leadership capacity are student achievement and the continued improvement of instruction of your teachers—and those are also the ALT's priorities. The following questions informed my writing:

- Does my leadership team function as a team in the truest sense of the word, or are we simply a collection of individuals?
- Are the priorities of my leadership team competing, or is it understood that, after student safety, student achievement and the continued improvement of instruction are our main priorities?

- Do the members of my leadership team possess the skill sets needed to be proficient instructional leaders?
- Are we as a leadership team continually collaborating on what effective pedagogy looks like?
- What is the mission of my school, and is it known and embraced by my leadership team and the entire school community?
- What is the vision of my school, and is it known and embraced by my leadership team and the entire school community?
- What are the academic goals and objectives of my school, and are they known and embraced by my leadership team and the entire school community?
- To what extent does my leadership team engage in ongoing school-level planning?
- What programs and activities that help deter undesirable student behaviors does my leadership team have in place?
- In what ways does my leadership team keep parents and key members of the community engaged in our work?

Does My Leadership Team Function as a Team in the Truest Sense of the Word, or Are We Simply a Collection of Individuals?

Whether it be the culture or any other aspect of the school, the leadership must function as a team in the truest sense of the word. The relationships that the team members have with one another are of paramount importance. The team cannot be a collection of leaders with their own agendas. That would translate to each member of the ALT functioning as leaders of portions of the school and never coming together as one team leading one school. For example, in a medium to large middle school, each grade level is led by an assistant principal, and in a high school, by an assistant principal—and this makes sense to me. Many large schools need to be reduced in size by becoming schools within schools. The problem is when they are solely schools within schools and not looked upon or treated as one school. Despite the fact that each administrator leads a particular grade level and has enormous responsibility in that capacity, the individual administrators should be functioning as a team and not solely as leaders of their respective grade levels. This requires ongoing collaboration, coordination, cohesion, and articulation between the ALT members led by the principal.

As schools are quite busy places, it is conceivable that in schools where there are leadership teams, team members can go days without seeing one another beyond passing each other in the hallways. Now imagine that all of the assistant principals are addressing discipline all day within their respective grade levels, visiting classrooms is an aberration, and formative pre- and post-observation conversations are nonexistent. This reality *begs* for the team to collaborate daily to compare notes and brainstorm to identify why these infractions continually occur and what measures need to be taken to shift the culture of the school to significantly decrease the time that the members of the ALT spend on discipline. As it stands, addressing undesirable student behavior *is* the prevailing culture. It begs for the ALT to have frank, and perhaps uncomfortable, discussions about the fact that the culture of the school is the primary impediment to real and ongoing instructional leadership—and the roles that the individual team members may play in perpetuating the problem. This is where the discomfort comes in, but it's necessary discomfort.

Meaningful change often requires tough, bold, honest, and uncomfortable conversations. A positive pivot in school culture is not going to occur magically or because you wish it to, and it's certainly not going to occur by continuing to have ALT members spend entire days addressing discipline. The ALT cannot embody effective instructional leadership and coaching if it is inundated by discipline and other ancillary aspects of school life. For example, if teachers are sending a steady stream of students to the office and you're not in the classrooms to observe the dynamics of the classrooms (to understand *why* students are being sent to you), you are not in a position to coach the teachers on how not to rely on administration to address discipline or provide them with strategies to prevent the occurrences of disciplinary infractions. If you are *in your office* reacting to the concerns of the teachers *from your office* instead of being in the classroom, that's unfortunate and counter to how a member of an ALT should lead.

I would be remiss if I didn't share a word on the dynamics of the ALT. If the team is going to function optimally, certain structures, systems, practices, guidelines, and understandings that will ideally result in the establishment of your ALT's core beliefs, core values, and core guiding principles as a team should be put in place. That is, the following must be established: professionalism; a bond; trust; a commitment to the team and to one another; confidence in the team and in one another; a defined purpose for existing; a defined mission; a defined vision; goals and objectives; an urgency to be effective as a team; rapport; relationships; attention to detail; a work ethic; team character; team chemistry; an environment of mutual support; persistence and perseverance; resilience of each team member and the team as a whole; team competency and credibility; integrity; systems, procedures, and practices, including the length of meetings and expectations regarding how team members will engage with one another; and an environment where each team member's ideas, perspectives, suggestions, as well as transparency and vulnerability, will be respected. There must also be a focus on student achievement; sustaining continued improvement of instruction; and establishing, building, nurturing, and sustaining a culture of instructional leadership. In other words, building a team requires a great deal of input and commitment from each member of the team.

Are the Priorities of My Leadership Team Competing, or Is It Understood That, After Student Safety, Student Achievement and the Continued Improvement of Instruction Are Our Main Priorities?

This question takes me right back to the dynamics of the team. The ALT is the head of the school. It's the think tank. It embodies the overall leadership of the building and sets the tone for who you are as a school. The school goes as the leadership goes. When the ALT and the school are rowing in opposite directions, chaos sets in. When the members of the ALT are rowing in different directions, further chaos sets in.

The purpose of this book is to have you think critically about who you are as instructional leaders to help you pivot away from any counterproductive practices and toward practices that increase the probability of effective instructional leadership. With every step you take as a school leader, you've got to ask yourself,

- How is this step contributing to why the students are in the building in the first place?
- How is this step contributing to my primary purpose for the teachers I supervise, which is student achievement and the continued improvement of instruction?
- What is *my* value instructionally to the teachers *I* supervise?
- What is *our* value as a team instructionally to the teachers *we* supervise?

Let's look at the ALT again. It is very easy to come into educational leadership with a variety of different or competing agendas, goals, objectives, interests, and priorities. I was clear from day 1 as an assistant principal that student achievement and the continued improvement of instruction of my staff were my *priorities* although, as an assistant principal, discipline was going to be my *reality*. Making student achievement and the continued improvement of instruction of my staff my reality took time, but it was always at the forefront of my mind.

As a 5th grade teacher, my priority was student achievement, but my vehicle to get there was culturally relevant pedagogy that allowed my students to see themselves in their learning. My students were Black, and the city (East Orange) in which I taught—and where I was raised—was Black. The performance of my students was low, which was consistent with data on Black student achievement nationally. I was convinced, even before I began teaching, that if the students who were assigned to me were given instruction that spoke to who they were historically and culturally, they would outperform their peers. I was unwavering in this belief. I wasn't awarded school-level, district-level, county-level, and New Jersey State finalist for Teacher of the Year for nothing. I staunchly believed at my core that Black children could achieve at high levels when learning is culturally relevant, relatable, and identifiable. And that's precisely how I taught my students. I employed an interdisciplinary approach to instruction, which was a no-brainer for me. Make learning relevant, relatable, and identifiable, and the children will achieve.

When I became an administrator, I brought with me the approach, focus, commitment, mentality, belief, and value that I employed as a teacher. I was an assistant principal of a middle school in the district in which I taught, just one block away from my former school. Many of my former students attended my new school. The principal and I were committed to student achievement, but our vehicles to get there were not at all aligned. We were a two-member team who saw the student achievement world very differently, and it showed in our professional relationship. Although we got along well personally, our conversations around education were practically nonexistent. Consequently, there wasn't a culture of instructional leadership.

I soon became the principal of the same middle school, and in each of the four schools that I led over the next 14 years, the administration teams comprised only two individuals—the principal and an assistant principal. Over the course of eight years as a middle school principal, my three assistant principals shared my unwavering core belief that culturally relevant pedagogy was the right vehicle for connecting academically with historically marginalized student populations. We were on the same page instructionally, which prevented competing priorities relative to our instructional core beliefs, core values, and core guiding principles.

I use this as an example relative to the potential for competing instructional perspectives, but the question asked in this section is about competing priorities within the team overall. Imagine an ALT where some members are locked in on student achievement and the continued improvement of instruction via cultural relevance and cultural responsiveness as their leadership priority, while others see order and discipline as the vehicle for improved academic outcomes and thereby spend all of their time in that capacity, at the expense of student achievement and the overall culture of the school. In this example, those who prioritize order and discipline believe that leading aggressively with a "no-nonsense," "zero-tolerance," "no-excuses" approach in an intimidating fashion via daily "putting out fires," "giving mini-sermons," calling parents, and imposing penalties such as detentions and suspensions will yield positive change. On the other hand, with a leader like myself who believes staunchly that if you "put the children in the lesson" and train the teachers (or hire teachers with similar outlooks), the behaviors will shift because the children have a purpose for learning, which in turn shifts the culture of the classroom. That's how I operated as an urban classroom teacher.

The translation here is that when this ALT comes together, the team is divided by competing priorities regarding what works to shift the culture. And when a team is divided, that divide has schoolwide implications. This is why the guidelines I provided under the first question of this chapter are so crucial. This doesn't mean that team members can't disagree, however. Disagreement is healthy; it stretches our thinking and allows us to grow. Data and evidence are key to disagreement. Solid evidence is crucial as team members must be able to back up their assertions.

I remain steadfast in my core belief that the primary purpose of the leadership team must be student achievement and the continued improvement of instruction. If that is going to be your leadership reality, the culture of "putting out fires" and "giving mini-sermons" to address individual student behaviors cannot be your leadership priority or your leadership norm. Shifting the culture of the classroom via strong and effective instructional leadership must be the priority of each member of your ALT so that your team becomes the instructional leaders your school needs you to be.

Do the Members of My Leadership Team Possess the Skill Sets Needed to Be Proficient Instructional Leaders?

You'll notice in this chapter that, up to this point, I have referenced student discipline but have not discussed a discipline program—and I won't. Why? Because discipline programs or penalties such as suspensions and detentions don't change student behaviors. Rather, it is the emphasis on school and classroom culture and all of its requisite tentacles, including restorative practices, that changes student behavior. A primary area of focus of the ALT must be the culture of the school. The overall environment of the school matters.

I wrote this book to encourage you to think critically about instructional leadership in general. But whether your direct supervision of teachers adds value to their pedagogical practices, I want to address the skill sets required for instructional leadership proficiency: verbal communication, nonverbal communication, and serving as resources.

Verbal Communication

Instructional leadership involves considerable one-on-one conversations, which requires proficiency in interpersonal communication and working with people. Your people skills must be sharp. Hold up your mirror and ask yourself the following questions about the relationships with the teachers you supervise:

- Do I demonstrate **approachability**? Your teachers must feel at ease approaching you about any and all issues regarding the classroom. How you respond will dictate your approachability.
- Do I demonstrate **relatability**? Your teachers must feel that you understand their world.
- Do I demonstrate **likability**? You must be able to present yourself such that teachers feel comfortable engaging with you.
- Do I demonstrate **dependability**? Your teachers must feel that you are truly there for them and in their classrooms.
- Do I demonstrate **reliability**? Your teachers must feel that they can always count on your input.

- Do I demonstrate **empathy?** Your teachers must feel that you truly understand their challenges.
- Do I demonstrate **equity?** Your teachers must feel that they are not being compared to their peers.
- Do I demonstrate **compassion?** Your teachers must feel that you genuinely care for them.
- Do I demonstrate **trustworthiness?** Your teachers must feel that interactions with you are confidential.
- Do I demonstrate **interest?** Your teachers must feel that you are genuinely interested in their professional growth and development.
- Do I demonstrate **patience?** Your teachers must feel that you completely understand that they can only progress at their own pace.
- Do I demonstrate **listening skills?** Your teachers must feel that they have your full attention when they are talking to you.
- Do I demonstrate **coaching skills?** Your teachers must feel that you are a proficient coach, including how you speak to them and your tone.
- Do I demonstrate **problem-solving skills?** Your teachers must feel that you are a resourceful problem solver.

How your teachers perceive you will be determined in large part by how you communicate with them verbally. Proficiently communicating verbally with teachers in your capacity as a coach is necessary for meetings. Poor communication skills can derail the entire intent of the coaching process. Therefore, an agenda item must be the importance of instructional leaders' proficiency in interpersonal communications.

Nonverbal Communication

Nonverbal communication is as important to leadership as verbal communication. While we are typically much more conscious of our verbal communication than we are of our nonverbal communication, our nonverbal communication matters as well. That being the case, hold up your mirror once again, and ask yourself the following about the relationships with the teachers you supervise.

What message does my presence communicate? We can be very intentional about a message we want to convey, but the message can get lost if our presence conflicts with it. We must always be mindful of how our presence is being interpreted.

Does my presence communicate leadership? If I spoke my mind blatantly on this one, my intent might be obscured. So I will instead simply say that if you are the leader of a school, look like you are the leader of a school. If you look like someone other than the leader of a school, whatever it is that you look like is the message being conveyed to your entire school community.

Does my posture communicate leadership? Your posture is a great communicator. Be certain that your posture delivers the intended message to your teachers. Body language is a powerful communicator, and you want to be sure that your body language is aligned with your intended meaning.

What messages do my facial expressions convey? This is a big one. You could be saying all the right things, but your face could be saying something dramatically different. You must ensure your words and your facial expressions are aligned. In other words, the teacher may not be able to hear you because your facial expressions are obscuring the message.

How do I make good use of eye contact? Remember that we're not all the same. While we talk a great deal about eye contact being essential, eye contact relative to what you represent as a leader, your overall presence, and your demeanor can be intimidating. Eye contact that is unintentionally intimidating and overwhelming can potentially lead to a breakdown in communications with teachers. You must be intentional about getting to know your teachers to know how to effectively communicate with them verbally and nonverbally, because they are all different inclusive of the effects of eye contact.

Do my hand gestures enhance my nonverbal communication? I unintentionally communicate with my hands. I believe, however, that it enhances my communication. I bring it up here because I want to caution you that it could detract from your verbal message. It's another area that you should pay attention to.

The topics a leadership team can discuss are endless, which is why it is so crucial that you take your roles as members of the ALT seriously and meet regularly. Side and passing conversations aren't enough. There is a need for regular and ongoing conversations about everything that falls under your leadership, including discussion of nonverbal communication. It's one of those things that an ALT might overlook because it may not be perceived as a big-ticket item, but sometimes, things that seem incidental can have buildingwide implications. An ALT with members whose verbal and nonverbal communication skills are deficient is actually a big deal. For example, a member of the team may be unable to connect with a teacher and can't figure out why, and it could boil down to the manner in which they communicate nonverbally. The lack of these skills could potentially drive a wedge between the leadership and staff and result in a breakdown in your instructional leadership. It's an absolutely essential topic for the ALT to delve into.

Serving as Resources

While verbal and nonverbal communication with teachers are critical components toward your proficiency as coaches, serving as resources is equally critical. Hold up your mirror one last time, and ask yourself the following questions.

As a leadership team, are we good resources? In other words, is your ALT a good resource for establishing a culture of instructional leadership? Do teachers view your leadership team as a resource? As instructional coaches, the teachers you supervise must view you as resources. You must know what you're talking about so you can add value to their pedagogy. As a leadership team, you must be instructional resources for the entire school community and for each other, for the good of the individual team members and the team as a whole. Each member brings their own unique experiences, background, knowledge base, understandings, and skill sets to the team. When all of these experiences, backgrounds, knowledge bases, understandings, and skill sets come together with fidelity and intentionality, it's a win for individuals and the leadership team overall, and it culminates in a win for the entire school community.

What do we as a leadership team have to offer to our teachers relative to instructional strategies? It's one thing to observe a lesson and conclude that it didn't meet its intended objectives or expectations, but what strategies do we as instructional leaders bring to the table to make the lesson effective? As an instructional leader, there must be more to your repertoire than critique. You must be a problem solver and solution-driven.

What do we know about the students our teachers teach? As you grow as an instructional leader, a part of that growth is developing a solid familiarity of who the students who are assigned to your teachers are academically. This understanding is important. But to go further, what do the data say about them within a particular content area or skill area? What are their strengths? What are their deficiencies? As an effective instructional leader, student academic data must be an integral area of concentration for you as well. And be mindful that student data won't be limited to information on academic performance (as attendance and discipline will affect academic performance). Academic, attendance, and discipline data are equally import- ant for the ALT. The review and analysis of student data must also be an integral component of your overall leadership team discussions, which, in turn, place you in a better position to assist your teachers with the analysis of their data.

What do we know about the content areas our teachers teach? I will make the argument until I can't make it anymore: It is a plus when instructional leaders have a proficiency in a content area, but it would be quite unrealistic to expect you to be proficient in all content areas. What you must be proficient in is pedagogy. If you don't know effective pedagogy, you are not in a position to coach a teacher pedagogically. An advan- tage of having a functioning ALT is that the chances are good that the individual members may be stronger in a given con- tent area than you are. That being the case, in a leadership team meeting, members can share strategies based on their different content-area backgrounds and levels of expertise.

What do we know about effective pedagogy? To build on the previous question, effective pedagogy is an ongoing topic of discussion for the leadership team. Members have the oppor- tunity to discuss effective pedagogy of the teachers they super- vise. Subsequently, they can schedule walkthroughs of those classrooms so that all team members can observe the particular teacher and determine how the teacher's pedagogy might be transferable and benefit their colleagues.

Do the teachers feel that the members of the leadership team are supportive of their needs? This question requires that I write a bit more than I did in the previous sections, as I'm thinking about all the teachers I meet throughout the United States who share with me privately during breaks and over lunch that they feel overwhelmed by the work. I'm think- ing about the crisis that we face as a profession relative to the volume of teachers who are leaving the profession, not because of salary and economics but because of the increased pressures and demands associated with their work at the school, district, and state levels. I'm thinking about the teachers who tell me that the challenges of managing a classroom, inclusive of student behaviors, have gotten harder post-pandemic. I'm thinking about the teachers who have expressed losing their joy of teaching because of the culture of standardized testing. I'm thinking about the teachers who feel overwhelmed by aggressive, disrespectful, or disengaged parents. I'm thinking about the teachers who have expressed that staff morale is so low that the school is just not a fun place to work. I'm thinking about the teachers who feel unsupported by administration. I could go on and on, but I will stop there.

As of this writing (2024), we are in a crisis relative to teacher shortages in many urban and rural schools in particular across the United States. Teachers have left in droves since the pandemic. Education has shifted dramatically from what we knew it to be before the pandemic (which doesn't translate to me saying it was better pre-pandemic). The children have changed in so many ways, and as a result, many teachers feel drained, exhausted, burnt out, stressed, and depressed and are continually concerned about their mental and emotional well-being. This is in large part due to the fact that the strategies that worked for them pre-pandemic are not necessarily working for them the same way post-pandemic. (I frequently say to them that as the children changed, you must change along with them. The pre-pandemic "you" may no longer be applicable to the post-pandemic youngster.) The pressures and demands of the work can be so overwhelming for your teachers, and this is where you come in as a leadership team. Yes, you are feeling and experiencing the same pressures and demands as your teachers, and you, too, must be attentive to your own mental and emotional well-being. You, too, must seek support when and where needed. But the question here is about your teachers. Do you provide them with the support they need to stay fired up about their work? What does the support you provide look like? Do your teachers know that you are always there for them? It will be most challenging to lead them instructionally when the overall environment of your school is not conducive to them bringing the energy, excitement, and enthusiasm for the work that you would want them to bring. Said differently, it will be most challenging to lead them instructionally when they have one foot out the door due to the culture of the school, the overall environment of the school, and the lack of support from administration.

You will recall that in the discussion of verbal communication I stated that you must be able to demonstrate *approachability, relatability, likability, dependability, reliability, empathy, equity, compassion, trustworthiness, interest, patience,* and *listening, coaching, and problem-solving skills.* Those all matter and contribute to a healthy school culture and teachers feeling that they are supported by administration.

Again, these are questions that the leadership team should regularly delve into as you accentuate school culture toward eliminating student discipline. They all speak to the culture of your school, the culture of your leadership team, and the culture of instructional leadership in your school.

As I close this section, as it relates to discipline, I will say it again: Students are not the problem. And again: Students are not the problem. It can be us, the leadership, who can be the problem when we do not have the necessary systems—one being the ongoing collaboration of the leadership team—in place to maximize the potential and productivity of the leadership team instructionally.

Are We as a Leadership Team Continually Collaborating on What Effective Pedagogy Looks Like?

In the previous section, I asked the question, "What do we know about effective pedagogy?" Here, I want to examine what the collaboration of the team might look like relative to effective pedagogy. It is not enough for the individual team members to have instructional mentalities, instructional work ethics, and an instructional focus in isolation of one another. You are in the same school—a school with common goals, objectives, and a mission and a vision. In other words, you all want the same thing. Therefore, your leadership can't be disjointed, disconnected, or detached from one another. Cohesion must be the goal. You must all be rowing in the same direction, which means that the collaboration of the ALT on instruction is essential, including the ongoing review of your district's instructional rubric and teacher evaluation instrument. Just as I mentioned that a given leader on the team may be stronger in a particular content area than others, the same holds true that there are aspects of pedagogy that one member of the team could be quite conversant in where another member has limited familiarity. This limited knowledge from the one member could have adverse implications if this leader is an instructional leader of teachers (as you can only share what you know). When the ALT is collaborative on what effective pedagogy looks like, there is a higher probability that the leadership will be quite knowledgeable in all things pedagogy.

As principal of your school, the collaboration of your leadership team on effective pedagogy just makes sense. When I was a principal, one thing that was extremely glaring to me about my teaching staff was that my younger teachers who had recently gone through their preservice training were so much more knowledgeable about current pedagogical practices than their veteran peers. Well, the same applies when you have an ALT whose age range is large. There's a possibility that the younger administrators are more knowledgeable of current pedagogical practices than the veteran members of the team. Through collaboration, the veteran administrators are in a position to learn from their younger peers. And as the veteran leaders have wisdom and experiences that the younger administrators lack, the benefits of the collaboration are dual. As the principal, the initiation of the leadership collaborations is in your hands. The sky is the limit as to what these collaborations look like, including the leadership team participating in article studies, blog post studies, and book studies; listening to podcasts; viewing livestreams; and attending conferences, institutes, and academies, to name a few. The bottom line is that the team is functioning as a team in the truest sense of the word and in this case has laser-like focus on effective pedagogical practices. I might add that your instructional coaches could and should be a part of this particular collaboration with the leadership team. They bring important pedagogical insights to the discussions in their capacities as instructional coaches.

Before moving on, you will notice that the word *collaboration* was used several times in this section. In other words, I put a lot of emphasis on the members of the ALT working together, collaboratively. This should result in an ALT that works like a well-oiled machine as accountability partners and thought partners on all things, school leadership in general, and instructional leaders in particular. When your team member holds you accountable or shares your thoughts, the entire school community wins.

What Is the Mission of My School, and Is It Known and Embraced by My Leadership Team and the Entire School Community?

Another critical area of focus for the leadership team relative to shaping culture and giving far less energy to student discipline is the intentionality of the mission and the intentionality of the vision of the school. I will focus here on the mission (and on vision in the next question).

First, notice that I said "the intentionality of the mission." In other words, most schools have a mission statement posted somewhere, but that's not good enough. To confront student discipline as a school community or a school family, the intent must be to *live* the mission. What I mean by this is the way I define *mission* in the first place: who the school is and what the school is about. When I am working with a school staff or school leadership team, I typically ask, "Who are you as a school, and what are you about as a school?" Or I will simply ask them to recite the school mission statement in unison. In most places that I go, this translates to dead silence, with many looking to their phones and laptops, which I immediately discourage. I tell those with whom I'm working that if you don't have a mission statement or the mission is not known, based on the definition, as a school, you are no one and you "ain't about nothing" (and I deliberately stated "ain't about nothing" to bring the point home).

Now I know this sounds cruel, but that is the intent. I want to make the point that either the absence or the lack of awareness of the mission is deeply problematic. Imagine that discipline is an issue that prevents you from being the instructional leader you need to be while your students walk into a mission-less school every morning. Do you see the problem?

The mission must be sewn into the fabric of the school and recited as a school community as regularly as possible, such as in the following ways:

- After the flag salute while all are still standing during the morning announcements.
- To open assemblies and principal's meetings.
- To open staff meetings.
- To open parent meetings.

Also, randomly ask students to recite it. This is what I mean by the "intentionality of the mission statement." It shouldn't just be posted on a wall. It's bigger than that. It's who your school is and what it is about—what it represents. Now keep in mind that the mission statement doesn't have to be a long, lofty paragraph. In fact, I discourage this. Instead, it should comprise one powerful or potent sentence that captures who you are and what you are about as a school. The bottom line, though, is when the mission statement is either nonexistent or unknown, it translates to a mission-less school, and when children enter a mission-less school, issues of student discipline can abound. When the mission statement is unknown, it essentially doesn't exist.

As a leadership team, this is yet another responsibility that falls on your shoulders. You must ensure that the mission drives everything about your school. If the current mission statement is outdated or obsolete, then you must engage in discussion as a team about revising it. You might even write a draft and present it to your staff for input. If staff are going to embrace it, they must feel that they are a part of it. Soliciting their input gives them the opportunity to share their thoughts and ideas. Everyone may not want to be involved, but you would have sought their input. To establish a culture of instructional leadership, the mission of your school can never be overstated. It absolutely matters and is, therefore, a core responsibility of the ALT.

What Is the Vision of My School, and Is It Known and Embraced by My Leadership Team and the Entire School Community?

Imagine a school where everyone shows up and works hard but where you are going is unknown and undefined or you're just going around and around in circles. In other words, you all are present but not everyone knows or embraces the destination. This is a school that lacks vision. To reduce disciplinary issues, where your school is going must be known and embraced by all.

Much of what I said about the mission applies to the vision. I always ask my audiences what the vision is of their school, and in most cases, they do not know, which translates to it not existing. My response to them is that a school without a vision is a perpetually stagnant school or a school in perpetual motion going nowhere. There's no big picture, just a wish, hope, or fantasy. Using my earlier vernacular, I tell them that a school without a vision is "a school that ain't going nowhere." As with the mission, the vision should be recited as a school community as regularly as possible:

- After the flag salute and mission, while all are still standing during the morning announcements.
- Along with the mission, to open assemblies and principal's meetings.
- Along with the mission, to open staff meetings.
- Along with the mission, to open parent meetings.

As with the mission, students should be randomly asked to recite it. As a leadership team, you must review the vision and determine whether the existing one is still relevant—if one exists at all. If it doesn't, you as a team must devise one powerful and potent sentence. Then, as with the mission statement, present it to staff for their input, again allowing them to be a part of the process.

As it relates to discipline, issues of discipline are inevitable when a student body walks into a vision-less school every day. The school's vision is therefore another integral component of the work of the ALT. In other words, in that conference room where the leadership team is meeting, there can't be confusion about where the school is headed under your leadership. As the mission and vision statements should literally be posted all over the school, one of the places they should be posted is wherever the leadership team meets. The mission and the vision of the school should drive the work of the ALT while also serving as a foundation for everything instructional.

What Are the Academic Goals and Objectives of My School, and Are They Known and Embraced by My Leadership Team and the Entire School Community?

As a speaker who practically lives on the road, I drive rental cars more often than I drive my own car. Because I drive so many rentals, when I jump into my rental cars on my way to an engagement, it is all too common for me to start driving before I realize I have no idea where I am going. In other words, I start driving as if I know where I'm going, but I don't. I soon realize I need to activate the navigation system. That got me thinking about schools that operate without their own navigation systems. When you are leading a school and the school-level academic goals are unknown by your school community, you are leading an aimless school. It doesn't matter that an ALT has high standards and expectations if only they know them. It doesn't matter that an ALT has developed a mission and vision statement if only they know them. It doesn't matter that an ALT knows the school-level goals and objectives inside and out if only they know them. The academic goals and objectives must be known and ultimately embraced by all to provide the entire school with targets to aim for. Imagine trying to reduce discipline in a school that doesn't provide targets. If those targets do not exist, the students will create their own—which will invariably result in an endless stream of disciplinary referrals.

This is the role and responsibility of the leadership team, too. Imagine that the goals and objectives exist but you are the only ones who know them and can recite them. Then as you examine your school's academic data, you see that your school is falling far short of expectations or benchmarks. My question to you is, Are your teachers and students cognizant of your school's academic expectations and benchmarks relative to its goals and objectives? If not, it points to a huge hole in the role of the ALT. The academic goals and objectives must be front and center in your school and among your leadership team. As a leadership team, it is imperative that you brainstorm and strategize on how you will ensure that your school's academic goals and objectives are known and embraced by your entire school community as targets to aim for. That translates, for example, to the administrative leaders meeting with students by grade level on an ongoing basis to keep them informed and focused on your school's big picture goals and objectives. This also allows your students to see the members of the leadership team as educators and school leaders, not just disciplinarians. The significance of this cannot be overstated relative to the transformation of the culture of the school in general and the establishment of a culture of instructional leadership in particular.

To What Extent Does My Leadership Team Engage in Ongoing School-Level Planning?

Chances are good that, in the summer, you review and modify your school improvement plans for the forthcoming school year. While this is good and necessary, it's not enough. There must be a correlation between your school improvement plans and your effectiveness as instructional leaders, so the school improvement plan must be a living document, not a compliance document. If it is a living document, it will regularly inform your practice as an instructional leader. If, however, it is a compliance document, it will in all likelihood be detached from your practice as an instructional leader. In some places, it will sit on a shelf and collect dust. But here's the connection relative to discipline: I am certain that your school improvement plan will address student discipline, and as I outlined throughout this chapter, effective instructional leadership drives school culture, while school culture allows for instructional leadership. As I am prone to say, school culture is a reflection of school leadership. Student disciplinary infractions become the intended consequence in this regard when disciplinary referrals, instead of culture, are the focus for reducing undesirable behaviors.

At the core of all of this is ongoing school improvement planning led by the ALT. To that end, what does your school improvement plan comprise? Is your school improvement plan a living document or a compliance document? What role does your school improvement plan play in your ongoing leadership team meetings? To what extent is instructional leadership addressed in your school improvement plan? To what extent are the establishment and the development of a culture of instructional leadership addressed in your school improvement plan? To what extent are school and classroom culture addressed in your school improvement plan? To what extent did the leadership team engage in the development of the school improvement plan? To what extent is the school leadership team intimately familiar with the school improvement plan? The correlation between the school improvement plan and your effectiveness as instructional leaders is of paramount importance.

What Programs and Activities That Help Deter Undesirable Student Behaviors Does My Leadership Team Have in Place?

The foundation of your leadership team is planning. Again, if student discipline is preventing you from being the instructional leader your school requires that you be, what plans do you have to shift your leadership reality? I work with a lot of assistant principals and aspiring assistant principals, and in the early part of our session, I say to them, "Imagine you were the principal of your current school. What types of programs and activities that don't exist would you put in place?" I'm now asking you, as a member of your school's ALT, given the current landscape of your school, what types of programs and activities that don't exist do you need to put in place?

In many instances, undesirable student behaviors boil down to a lack of programming and activities that interest your students. Everyone's not going to make the athletic teams. What else is in place that every student in the building has an opportunity to participate in? A true student-centered school will always put students first. Are you a students-first school, and if so, what is the evidence? As your team comes together for its regular afternoon meetings, discussions on the programs and activities of your school for students should be ongoing. What types of programs and activities do you already have in place? Are there criteria for participation? Are there programs and activities in place for students of all academic achievement levels? Is there a marketing or incentive campaign to attract students to the various programs and activities offered? Are there programs that should be in place but have not yet been instituted? If so, what are they, and what's the holdup? A wide range of programs and activities for students is an additional contributor to a positive school culture.

This is yet another topic that the ALT should discuss on an ongoing basis.

In What Ways Does My Leadership Team Keep Parents and Key Members of the Community Engaged in Our Work?

Another important function of your leadership team toward establishing a culture of instructional leadership is parental and community engagement. Your school is not an island and can never operate as one. It is a critical part of a larger community. It is one of the institutions in the community that educates its future. But what if a significant portion of the student body is either underperforming because of insufficient instructional practices or exhibiting undesirable behaviors because of a counterproductive classroom culture that result in trips to your office, which in turn keep you confined to your office addressing discipline? In keeping with the same line of questioning, what is the relationship between your school and the surrounding community? Is your school embraced by the surrounding community? Does your school feel that it is a part of the surrounding community? Does your school contribute to the advancement of the surrounding community relative to the quality of education provided and the quality of young people it nurtures? These are important questions for the ALT to ponder and examine.

Let's go further. In what ways does your school tap into members of the community to partner with your school for various programs? In what ways does your school tap into key members of your community, such as government officials, religious leaders, business owners, managers and executives, community leaders and advocates, or just ordinary folks who want to be involved with your school? Have you tapped into these valuable human resources? I have found that communities are replete with people who want to help but have never been approached. They may not take the initiative, but they want to be of service and are waiting and hoping that the school will reach out to them. As the leader of your team, you must explore options to engage the community to get the word out about working with your school. Once again, we're talking about shifting the culture. The ALT must regularly collaborate to make the idea of a cultural shift become the school's reality. As the culture shifts, you are in position to think realistically about a culture of instructional leadership. But as long as the ALT is bombarded with matters unrelated to instruction, establishing a culture of instructional leadership is going to be a long way off. In other words, it will be very difficult to establish a culture of instructional leadership within a culture that is counterproductive and toxic.

Parents are also key members of the community. They are more than just the parents of your students; there's more to them. The question therefore is, How are you tapping into parents? You have greater access to them *because* they are the parents of your students. Your relationships with them can extend beyond that of principal and parent. Again, your leadership team has to spearhead this initiative. In other words, ongoing agenda items must include parental and community engagement to create a buildingwide culture conducive to high academic performance where student discipline is minimal and consequently instructional leadership and coaching are optimal.

Closing Thoughts on Assistant Principals

To close out this chapter, I want to highlight a key member of the ALT—the assistant principal or assistant principals.

For those of you who know my work, particularly since 2020, you know that I place a great deal of emphasis on the assistant principalship. I firmly believe that the assistant principalship is "the most misunderstood and underutilized position in all of education." Throughout my travels, I have concluded that there is much confusion in the United States around how best to utilize the AP position. I cringe when I see assistant principals relegated to being full-time disciplinarians. If that person doesn't supervise or evaluate teachers, I can live with it. But if that person supervises and evaluates teachers *and* spends the majority of their days disciplining students, I know that the coaching is minimal and consequently the evaluations lack substance. In this scenario, the children are being shortchanged. The assistant principal is a vitally important member of the ALT. I implore you to ask yourself the following questions:

- Do the climate and culture of my school allow my APs to be instructional leaders and coaches?
- Do my APs bring an instructional mentality, instructional work ethic, and instructional focus to their leadership?
- Do I bring an instructional mentality, instructional work ethic, and instructional focus to my supervision of my APs?

Let's explore all three.

Do the Climate and Culture of My School Allow My APs to Be Instructional Leaders and Coaches?

I want to once again draw your attention to the climate and culture of your school. First, for clarity, rather than use the scholarly definitions of *climate* and *culture*, I will use the simplified definitions that I have used throughout my career. When I say climate, I am simply referring to the *mood* of the school and of the classroom. Just as people have moods, places have collective moods when there are people in them. You walk into a restaurant, it has a mood. You walk into a store, it has a mood. You walk into a sports arena, it has a mood. You walk into a school, it has a mood. And when you walk into a classroom, you guessed it—it has a mood. It's very easy to gauge the mood of a place. You literally feel it when you are in the midst of the environment or even when you walk in. As it relates to our discussion, the moods of the school and the classroom matter.

I've always contended that the mood of the school is a direct reflection of the leadership of the building, and the mood of the classroom is a direct reflection of the teacher. Think of people and their moods. We tend to gravitate to people who bring a mood of energy and positivity versus people who bring a mood of gloom and negativity. Schools are the same way. When the energy is high and the atmosphere is positive, people tend to want to know what's going on in that school. When the energy is high and the atmosphere is positive, there's typically a correlation in that particular climate—between the mood and academic performance. The mood matters, and it is a direct reflection of the school's leadership.

My definition of *culture* is simply "the way we are living within the school, the *lifestyle* of the school." Referring to the examples of a restaurant, a store, and a sports arena, you walk into a restaurant and it has a culture. The food, the service, and the culture will determine whether you will return. The food and the service may be great, but the culture could have you saying, "This isn't the environment for me." The same applies to the store, the sports arena, or any public venue into which you venture. The culture matters. Culture matters in schools and classrooms as well. Schools cannot perform at optimal levels when the culture is incompatible with the goals, objectives, mission, and vision. They must be in sync if the school is going to perform at the levels that you envision. And as I stated regarding the school's climate, the school's culture is a direct reflection of the leadership of the building.

Let's now address the question posed: "Do the climate and culture of my school allow for my assistant principals to be instructional leaders and coaches?"

In my consulting capacity, I visit a ton of schools on school days. Regardless of my purpose for being in the building, I always gauge the climate and the culture upon entering the building to assess whether it feels conducive to instructional leadership. In a building that is calm throughout the morning, there's no doubt that the culture lends itself to the leadership being the instructional leaders the school requires. However, when I enter that school where there's chaos and security is moving about quickly, students are in the halls, the main office lobby is crowded with parents and students, there's constant communication on the walkie-talkies, and so on, it's pretty safe to assume that instructional leadership is not the norm in this environment.

Although I have described an extreme situation, the point I'm making is that the vehicle to being allowed to be the instructional leader you desire to be is the climate and culture of the school. Your leadership team must spearhead the effort to ensure that the climate and culture of your school are conducive to you having the time and the space to lead instructionally. You can never have an "it is what it is" mentality regarding a counterproductive climate and culture. No. You and your APs within your leadership have great influence over your school's climate and culture. And if you feel otherwise, you may need to rethink why you pursued school leadership. Your assistant principals must be able to lead the teachers that they supervise instructionally. Anything less and children will suffer. The role the ALT plays in establishing and building a culture of instructional leadership must be an ongoing conversation in your meetings.

Do My APs Bring an Instructional Mentality, Instructional Work Ethic, and Instructional Focus to Their Leadership?

I will say it again: The assistant principalship is the most misunderstood and underutilized position in all of education. I won't paint it with a broad brush, but I will say that there are far too many principals in the United States who were once assistant principals and the bulk of their work comprised the "big three": bus duty, cafeteria duty, and discipline. When these assistant principals eventually became principals and inherited their assistant principals, they utilized them the way they were utilized because that's what they knew. That's how they were trained. This is how I and countless others came up the ranks. For the sake of transparency, I'm letting you know that on my first day as an assistant principal, I did bus duty, did cafeteria duty, assigned detention, and suspended a student. Ouch!

My question to you then is, Do your assistant principals, under your stewardship, bring an instructional mentality to their leadership? Do your assistant principals, under your stewardship, bring an instructional leadership work ethic to their leadership? Do you monitor your assistant principals relative to their instructional leadership? Have you set standards and expectations for your assistant principals relative to their instructional leadership? Do you regularly meet with your assistant principals other than in leadership team meetings to gauge their progress as instructional leaders? Do your assistant principals regularly attempt to engage you in instructional leadership discussions? If so, are you receptive to these discussions? Do you initiate conversations about instruction with your assistant principals? Are these conversations normal and natural to your relationship, or are they forced or even anomalies? In other words, are the conversations with your assistant principals typically about teaching and learning in the classroom, or are they more about detention and suspension data and other negative indicators? Is it possible that your assistant principals could possess instructional mentalities that have been suppressed because this is not who you are as the principal of the school? For example, I talk basketball, but not with everyone. I talk basketball with people I perceive have an interest in talking basketball. If you, the principal, in fact have an instructional mentality but you perceive your assistant principal as more of a disciplinarian, chances are that you may be limited in your instructional or even educational discussions with your assistant principal, and this must change.

These are all questions that you should ponder relative to who your assistant principals are, what their focus is, and how they are being utilized by you. They are also questions relative to gauging who you are relative to your assistant principals in their instructional leadership capacities. Even in challenging school environments, your students deserve and require leaders who bring an instructional mindset and instructional work ethic to their leadership. And the climate and the culture of the school plays a major role in who you are as a team of leaders overall. Your assistant principals are integral parts of the ALT. They are educators. They are instructional leaders. They cannot contribute to the meeting instructionally if instruction is not what they do. If discipline is their primary role, that is what they are going to bring to the table.

Climate and culture matter, and that is a topic that the leadership team can never exhaust.

Do I Bring an Instructional Mentality, Instructional Work Ethic, and Instructional Focus to My Supervision of My APs?

In no way can you expect your assistant principals to be who you are not. If your expectation is that assistant principals are going to be solid instructional leaders of the teachers they supervise, you as the principal must demonstrate the same commitment to the teachers you supervise. You are the school's leader and must set the example. If your assistant principals bring an instructional mentality to their leadership that does not correlate with an instructional work ethic, chances are this is in line with the prevailing culture of the building. In other words, the culture is counterproductive, dysfunctional, or toxic. This results in a never-ending cycle of focusing on the consequences of a situation as opposed to the cause. Culture is everything, which means that, as it relates to your school, attention to detail must be the focus to lead the effort of molding, shaping, and crafting the culture of the school into what is best for children.

Everything mentioned begins with you. As the leader of your school, it is imperative that you bring an instructional mentality to your leadership team. This way it is clear through your conversations, meetings, and discussions that instruction is who you are and instruction is what you are about. As the leader of your school, it is imperative that you demonstrate an instructional work ethic to your leadership team, which will make clear that instruction is who you are and what you are about.

As the leader of your school, it is imperative that you bring a focus on instruction to your leadership team. This way, it is clear that instruction is who you are and what you are about. As the leader of your school where goals, objectives, a mission, and a vision drive your focus on instruction, as it relates to your relationship with and your supervision of your assistant principals, you must think and work instructionally, and you must commit to instruction. To that end, as the principal of your school, do you bring an instructional mentality to your assistant principals? Do you demonstrate an instructional work ethic for your assistant principals? Does your leadership embody an instructional focus for your assistant principals? Is instructional leadership at the core of your leadership, and is it evident to your assistant principals?

It's a Lot, I Know, but It's Designed to Help You

Admittedly, I have in this chapter put a lot on the plate of the leadership team. This chapter alone has probably potentially increased the workload of quite a few leadership teams out there. But as you increase your workload in the functions of the leadership team, it is my hope that there will be a corresponding decrease in noninstructional responsibilities. All leadership teams are different and therefore function differently. It is my hope that the questions and topics addressed here add value to your leadership team in general and your quest for a culture of instructional leadership in particular.

9

Maximizing Your
Instructional Coaches

*How am I using my instructional coaches,
and what measures have I put in place for
them to be optimally successful?*

As this chapter focuses solely on the role of the principal,
if you aspire to become a principal, this chapter is also
for you.

I have up to this point focused on you, the principal or the
assistant principal, in your capacity as instructional leader. As
I see it (and I may step on some toes here, but in a good, supportive way), a principal or an assistant principal who is not
an instructional leader is simply a building administrator or a
building manager. In other words, if you are not an instructional
leader, your connection to the instructional program at your
school does not go beyond high expectations and accountability
via evaluations. An instructional leader has a direct relationship
with teaching and learning, particularly with the teachers they
supervise—which makes you an educational leader as opposed
to an administrative leader.

In this chapter, I want to look at you not as an instructional leader but as who you are relative to how you engage and

use your instructional coaches to create instructional leadership synergy. You can't, and shouldn't, do this work alone. I understand that the composition of schools varies and that not all of you reading this book have assistant principals or instructional coaches. I, however, assume that the majority of you have at least one instructional coach for language arts and one for math, and therefore, I offer the self-reflective question that follows.

What Does My Training of and Collaboration with My Instructional Coaches Look Like?

Occasionally, I will speak at conferences where the audience comprises instructional coaches. When I interact with attendees during the breakout sessions, they typically have many questions and concerns. Among the concerns voiced by coaches in unionized districts (where instructional coaching can be quite challenging when the coaches and teachers are in the same bargaining unit) are the following:

- "Some of the teachers don't respect us in this capacity because they see us as peers."
- "We lack real authority because we are not administrators."

In all other districts, in addition to the foregoing, the following concerns are raised in the sessions:

- "Some of the teachers don't feel we are needed."
- "Some of the teachers don't want to be bothered with us."
- "Some of the teachers feel that we don't have anything substantive to offer."
- "Some of the teachers feel that our presence in their classrooms is an intrusion or a distraction."
- "Some of the teachers feel that meeting with us is a waste of their time."

- "Some of the teachers feel that since administration isn't in their classrooms, we shouldn't be in them either."
- "Some of the teachers can be disrespectful."
- "Some of the teachers feel they are beyond learning from us."
- "It can be challenging to forge relationships with some of the teachers because they don't trust us or the process."
- "Some of the teachers feel that we are reporting to administration on their performance in the classroom."

When I hear these concerns, my thoughts immediately go to culture. These concerns—particularly the last two—are impediments to a healthy culture of instructional coaching, and I'm led to conclude, based on what I've heard, that a culture for instructional coaches and instructional coaching is absent.

Let's look at three areas of focus toward improvement.

Transforming the School's Culture

If there is no culture for instructional coaching, instructional coaching is not going to happen. Period. As the principal of the school, you and your leadership team must lead the effort in establishing a culture of instructional coaching for your instructional coaches. Unlike leaders, instructional coaches do not possess administrative authority. Their ability to get results is not bolstered by a title. As a result, they proceed differently from you in those areas where your title gives you authority.

Let's look at staff meetings. What do they comprise? Are they administrative in nature? Are they top-down? Do administrators do all of the talking? Do you follow an agenda (a script) and strive to keep the meetings short?

Now imagine a staff meeting where the administrative aspects of the agenda have been reduced to an emailed staff bulletin, a large portion of the meeting is devoted to professional development with an emphasis on teaching and learning, and there is an ongoing focus on the vision of instructional coaching and the role of the instructional coaches. In an initial staff meeting, after you've provided an overview of your vision of what coaching via your instructional coaches in your school would look like, you turn the meeting over to the instructional coaches and allow them to elaborate on their roles, explain what instructional coaching is and what it is not, and allay any concerns teachers may have about nonadministrative instructional coaches.

It is important that the instructional coaches be thoroughly prepared for the initial meeting and all subsequent meetings where they are on the agenda. Preparation should include addressing how to handle staff objections during the Q&A in a professional and composed manner. They should relay both what content will be shared and how it will be shared. The teachers should leave the meetings feeling comfortable working with instructional coaches.

The instructional coaches will engage staff in a Q&A with the goal of listening to and responding to every concern raised by the teachers. A good practice would be having your coaches as fixtures on your staff meeting agendas (as they will likely have a lot of useful information to share).

Staff can in meetings study a brief article or blog post on the role of instructional coaches and transition to table and whole-group discussions on the role of the instructional coach in bringing about schoolwide clarity—which, along with understanding and trust, is part of an instructional coaching culture.

Instructional coaching is about nothing more than the pedagogical growth and development of the teachers in the building to maximize the academic potential of each of the students in the building. It's a grow ya, not a gotcha.

Training

As a principal, you can't just hire a candidate and, based on the strength of their pedagogy and content knowledge, expect them to be a proficient instructional coach. Coaching is a skill in and of itself. For instructional coaches to be effective, they will likely need to be trained. They will need to learn how to coach colleagues—their peers.

Toward making the instructional coaches beneficial to your school, training should include the following:

- How to approach, talk to, and work with teachers who are nonadministrative peers.
- How to position themselves as credible despite not being administrators.
- How to position themselves so that the teachers feel the value of the partnership.
- How to position themselves in ways that the teachers welcome them and their input.
- How to position themselves in ways that the teachers feel that their input is substantive and ongoing.
- How to position themselves in ways that the teachers don't feel that their presence in their classrooms is an intrusion or a distraction.
- How to position themselves in ways that the teachers don't feel that meeting with them is a waste of time.
- How to position themselves in ways that they are always respected and appreciated by the teachers.
- How to position themselves in ways that the teachers feel that they are growing professionally.
- How to position themselves in ways that trust is established and that the process is a grow ya, not a gotcha.

Collaboration

An earlier chapter discussed the collaboration and synergy of the administrative team. That collaboration, however, does not stop with the administrative team. Time must be built in for the instructional coaches. They have much to share, and their input must be valued.

Always bear in mind that although the instructional coaches regularly meet with the administrative team, they are not administrators. As it's easy for that line to get blurred, you must ensure that it doesn't. Your instructional coaches must never function in an administrative capacity. They do not have the authority to supervise or evaluate teachers; if and when teachers begin to perceive that they do, the entire process will collapse, and the culture of instructional coaching that you have built will cease to exist. The instructional coaches are partners and collaborators, not administrators. They should be included in leadership team meetings simply to share their progress and overall experiences, not to report on individual teachers. They should share their experiences as instructional coaches, including the progress they are making and the challenges they face. They should be at the top of the agenda and allotted a short period of time to present (as they are not administrators, their time in administrative leadership team meetings should be brief).

10

How You Are Perceived
Is Who You Are

*How do the teachers I supervise perceive
me as an instructional leader?*

This chapter is rooted in a question that I encourage you to
ask yourself regularly relative to who you are as an instructional leader in the eyes of the teachers you supervise.

Brand Identity and Brand Image

Your leadership brand identity—which you create or into which
you evolve—is essentially who and what you claim to be as a
leader in your school. It's how you see yourself and how you
want to be perceived by your school community.

As a principal, I was well aware of the various hats I wore.
But when it came to my leadership brand identity and how
I wanted to be seen by my students, only one hat mattered
to me: motivator. I wanted my students to see me as the person who fired them up and made them believe that anything
was possible.

On the flip side of the brand coin is brand image. Brand
image is essentially how you are being perceived by others. The

challenge is aligning your brand identity and your brand image.

As my leadership brand identity was motivator, it would have been problematic if my students perceived me as other than, or the antithesis of, a motivator. Fortunately for me, as I was a motivator in the eyes of my students, my leadership brand identity and my leadership brand image were in alignment.

Aligning Brand Image and Brand Identity: Critical Questions

It is typical for me when speaking to an audience of building leaders to ask those who consider themselves instructional leaders to raise their hands. Many hands go up. However, when I then ask to see the hands of those who feel that their teaching staff would view them as instructional leaders, fewer hands are raised. What this tells me is that many leaders are aware of the difference between their brand identities and their brand images.

If instructional leadership is indeed an important component of your leadership brand identity, you must be intentional about ensuring that your brand identity and your brand image are in alignment. Your teachers are not following who you *say* you are but who they *perceive* you to be—their image of you.

To facilitate alignment, ask yourself the following questions regarding how your teachers perceive you as an instructional leader:

- What would the narrative of the teachers I supervise be of me as an instructional leader?
- How am I currently being perceived by the teachers I supervise in my capacity as instructional leader?
- Can my teachers conclude that they are better teachers because of the relationship that they have with me?
- Who am I relative to the instructional growth and development of the teachers I supervise?

- Do the teachers I supervise perceive that I am an asset to their instructional practices and ongoing professional growth and development?
- Do the teachers I supervise perceive that my experience as a teacher adds value to their teaching?
- Do the teachers I supervise perceive that I share appropriate instructional strategies with them?
- Do the teachers I supervise perceive that I am well versed in good, sound pedagogy that benefits all learners?
- Do the teachers I supervise perceive that I offer a variety of instructional strategies that consider the varying academic needs of their students?
- Do the teachers I supervise perceive me as a source of sound instructional strategies?

These are important questions to regularly ask yourself relative to both who you are as instructional leader and how you are perceived as an instructional leader by the teachers you supervise.

Conclusion

Can I in good conscience refer to myself as an instructional leader in my school?

The 10 overarching questions around which this book is structured guided my thinking and my writing over the days and nights that I wrote it.

It is my sincere hope that these questions and the content that accompanies them are extremely beneficial to your leadership in general and your instructional leadership in particular. As you're now reading the Conclusion, I can safely assume that you have read the entire book. And because you've read the entire book, my culminating self-reflective question is, I believe, the most logical: "Can I in good conscience refer to myself as an instructional leader in my school?"

I've throughout the book said much about you and your team as instructional leaders. Although I am sure that much of the book has been affirming for you, it is my hope that you have been challenged by some of my thoughts, ideas, and past practices. As I've stated throughout the book, *instructional leadership must be at the core of your leadership existence and reality.* When it is not, ask yourself whether you can in good conscience refer to yourself as an instructional leader. But don't use the question as the be-all and end-all. Instead, use it as a bridge to what I consider to be the quintessential and most potent self-reflective question an instructional leader can ask: "What is my value instructionally to the teachers I supervise?"

Appendix:
Instructional Leadership
Blueprint

I consider "What is my value instructionally to the teachers I supervise?" to be the quintessential question that principals or assistant principals can ask themselves relative to instructional leadership. It is a derivative of my overall quintessential question for school leaders: "Is my school a better school because I lead it?" I encourage you to adopt, embrace, and take full ownership of both questions as sources of reflection throughout your career as a school leader.

Admittedly, instructional leadership is not easy, particularly in environments with competing challenges (such as a school whose culture doesn't align with the demands of effective instructional leadership). Instructional leadership isn't something that one can just jump into upon becoming aware of and understanding its significance. As indicated throughout this book, your effectiveness as an instructional leader and the overall culture of your school—which includes a culture of instructional leadership with your staff—must be in alignment.

Instructional leadership is an entity, an institution within your school. All institutions require a plan, strategy, or blueprint.

As an undergraduate who majored marketing, I learned a great deal about marketing plans. I was deeply immersed in the marketing program when I realized that education, not marketing, was my calling. Rather than end my marketing studies and start over, I brought the marketing program along with me into education. The result was the birth of several blueprints—school leadership, goal setting, equity, climate/culture, closing the attitude gap, and many others—and one aimed at instructional leadership. I thank God every day for leading me to marketing before I became an educator. I have no doubt that I would not have been the effective educator I was had I not studied marketing.

The Instructional Leadership Blueprint Detailed

The instructional leadership blueprint (ILB) is a plan for effective instructional leadership. You can make it yours and use it in conjunction with other thought leaders or accountability partners in your orbit (as discussed in Chapter 8).

Sections of the Instructional Leadership Blueprint

- **Situation analysis.** This is an analysis of who you are in real time as an instructional leader in your school. It answers the question "Where am I now?" By extension, the question "How did I get here?" is implied. This section of the blueprint requires brutal honesty on your part as to who you are right now as an instructional leader.
- **Goals.** This section of the ILB answers the question "Where am I going?" I have been a huge proponent of goal setting since my days as an undergraduate. Goal setting is not as simple as concluding that there are certain

goals you want to achieve, writing them down, and pursuing them. There's more to it than that. The situation analysis is vitally important to goal setting because it details your starting point. To set goals as an instructional leader, determining and analyzing your starting point is essential—and unavoidable. The situation analysis, like a GPS or navigation system in an automobile, is effective because it gives you directions based on your starting point (i.e., your current situation).

- **Strategy.** This section of your ILB answers the question "How will I get there?" This is where the rubber meets the road. It's one thing to list your wins, deficiencies, and the shifts you need to make. However, developing a detailed plan to achieve your goals is another thing. As is often said, "A goal without a plan is nothing but a wish." There must be a plan—a strategy—associated with the goals.

Subsections of Each Section in the Instructional Leadership Blueprint

- **Areas where I want to continue to grow (my wins).** Here is where you list everything that you are doing well relative to instructional leadership (e.g., "I am weekly coaching the number of teachers that I deem to be feasible"; "I am seeing the growth in the teachers I supervise who were struggling in different aspects of instruction"; "I have effectively led the effort of developing a well-functioning leadership team"). I begin with this subsection because it is very easy to lose sight of, forget, or take for granted your wins and instead harp on any challenges, obstacles, shortfalls, and deficiencies you may have. It serves as a reminder to recognize and acknowledge all the good you are doing that you may not give much thought or attention to. Your list should be lengthy. If you find that your list is relatively short, you have a lot of work to do. My second reason for including this subsection is a key word: *continue*. I want to encourage you to continue to grow and develop in areas in which you are already effective.

- **Areas where I need to improve (my deficiencies).** Here's where you list your deficiencies relative to instructional leadership. As you analyze your current situation, a complete list of your instructional leadership deficiencies is a must if you are going to correct them (e.g., "I don't have good chemistry with some of the teachers I coach"; "I don't consistently follow up with some of the teachers that I have observed in a timely manner"; "I don't consistently follow through after post-observation conversations"). The objective is to identify all of your deficiencies as an instructional leader so that you can correct them.

- **Areas where I need to make a pivot (a shift).** While the first two subsections are pretty much cut-and-dried, here you are asking yourself which practices that either once worked or never worked do you consider obsolete and need to purge from your instructional leadership practice (e.g., striving to consistently meet with a set number of teachers daily, striving to give each teacher the same amount of time in the pre-observation conversations, striving to visit each classroom for the same duration of time). Whatever that may be, you may have exhausted all attempts at improving in it and need to shift away from it.

The Instructional Leadership Blueprint Template

I. Situation Analysis (Where am I now?)

    A. Areas where I want to continue to grow (my wins)
        1.

        2.

        3.

    B. Areas where I need to improve (my deficiencies)
        1.

        2.

        3.

    C. Areas where I need to make a pivot (a shift)
        1.

        2.

        3.

Note: I included three items per section solely for the sake of brevity. The number of items listed is entirely based on what you come up with in your analysis of your current instructional leadership situation.

II. Goals (Where am I going?)

    A. Areas where I want to continue to grow (my wins)
        1.

        2.

        3.

    B. Areas where I need to improve (my deficiencies)
        1.

        2.

        3.

C. Areas where I need to make a pivot (a shift)
   1.

   2.

   3.

Note: Your goals should be directly tied to each of the wins, deficiencies, and shifts listed in your situation analysis. What's key here is the alignment of the two sections to keep your ILB organized.

III. Strategy (How will I get there?)

A. Areas where I want to continue to grow (my wins)
   1.

   2.

   3.

B. Areas where I need to improve (my deficiencies)
   1.

   2.

   3.

C. Areas where I need to make a pivot (a shift)
   1.

   2.

   3.

Note: You need to develop a detailed plan of action for *each item* listed in the Situation Analysis and Goals sections. A1 in your Situation Analysis section will align with A1 in the Goals and Strategy sections, B1 in your Situation Analysis section will align with B1 in the Goals and Strategy sections, C1 in your Situation Analysis section will align with C1 in the Goals and Strategy sections, and so on.

Here's what a completed Situation Analysis might look like that you may find helpful for developing the remainder of your blueprint.

Sample Instructional Leadership Blueprint

I. Situation Analysis (Where am I now?)

A. Areas where I want to continue to grow (my wins)

  1. I am coaching the number of teachers that I deem to be feasible each week.

  2. I am seeing the growth in the teachers that I supervise who were struggling in different aspects of instruction.

  3. I have effectively led the effort of developing a well-functioning leadership team.

B. Areas where I need to improve (my deficiencies)

  1. I don't have good chemistry with some of the teachers I coach.

  2. I don't consistently follow up with some of the teachers that I have observed in a timely matter.

  3. I don't consistently follow through after post-observation conversations.

C. Areas where I need to make a pivot (a shift)

  1. Striving to consistently meet with a set number of teachers daily.

  2. Striving to give each teacher the same amount of time in the pre-observation conversations.

  3. Striving to visit each classroom for the same duration of time.

Ways to Use the Instructional Leadership Blueprint

Keep in mind that you can use your ILB in one of several ways. You can develop it for monthly use (i.e., monthly assess your progress and revise your ILB), quarterly use (i.e., quarterly assess your progress and revise your ILB), or annual use (i.e., at the end of each year, revise your ILB based on your progress at the end of the school year after having monitored your progress throughout the course of the school year). Some of you would, I'm sure, find value in using your ILB weekly.

Bear in mind that this template is not limited to usage for instructional leadership. It can be used in all aspects of your leadership. In fact, when I was a teacher, my students were required to develop an ILB and review and revise it quarterly, which in this case was called the Goal-Setting Blueprint (GSB). The GSBs were written on large index cards and posted on a classroom wall, and I reviewed them with students individually. The positive effect that the GSB had on student achievement was immeasurable. I also used it all 14 years of my principalship, when the teachers and I reviewed the student-developed GSBs (also written on large index cards), which again greatly positively affected student achievement.

Implementation

Over the years, I've added a fourth section—Implementation—as a reminder that the implementation of your ILB must be ongoing. There's no template here. It's just a reminder of the significance of implementation and ongoing consistency.

Don't develop a blueprint that will just collect dust throughout the course of the school year. Your ILB should be a living document throughout your leadership tenure. It works—when used correctly and consistently. To that end, always maintain a spirit of walking in your plan while being consistent with your self-reflections, self-assessments, and self-adjustments while also striving for self-improvement, self-preservation, and self-care.

Bibliography

Edoho-Eket, R. (2023). *The principal's journey: Navigating the path to school leadership*. Author.

Harvey, R. (2023). *The playbook of principles for principals*. Wise Publications.

Jackson, M. (2024). *Essential systems for school success: An integrative organizational framework*. Kindle Direct Publishing.

Kafele, B. K. (2016). *The teacher 50: Critical questions for inspiring classroom excellence*. ASCD.

Kafele, B. K. (2019). *Is my school a better school because I lead it?* ASCD.

Kafele, B. K. (2020). *The assistant principal 50: Critical questions for meaningful leadership and professional growth*. ASCD.

Kafele, B. K. (2021). *The equity and social justice education 50: Critical questions for improving opportunities and outcomes for Black students*. ASCD.

Muhammad, A. (2009). *Transforming school culture: How to overcome staff division*. Solution Tree.

Muhammad, K. (2018). *Culturally responsive school leadership (race and education)*. Harvard Education Press.

Parker, D. (2024). *Be the driving force: Leading your school on the road to equity*. Solution Tree.

Schwanke, J. (2016). *You're the principal! Now what? Strategies and solutions for new school leaders*. ASCD.

Schwanke, J. (2020). *The principal reboot: 8 ways to revitalize your school leadership*. ASCD.

Stronge, J. H., & Xu, X. (2021). *Qualities of effective principals* (2nd ed.). ASCD.

Thomas-EL, S., Jones, J., & Vari, T. J. (2019). *Passionate leadership: Creating a culture of success in every school*. Corwin.

Turner, N. S. (2022). *Simply instructional coaching: Questions asked and answered from the field*. Solution Tree.

Whitaker, T. (2003). *What great principals do differently*. Eye on Education.

White, M., & Carter, D. L. (2021). *Leading schools in disruptive times: How to survive hyper-change*. Corwin.

Index

principals, assistant (*continued*)
  instructional focus, 125–128
  as instructional leaders and
    coaches, climate and culture
    allowing, 122–124
  instructional mentality, 125–128
  supervision, quality, 125–128
  vignette, 14
  work ethic, 125–128
principalship, pursuing the, 10–11,
  31–33
professional growth and development
  ensuring relevant, 87–88
  for instructional leaders, 24,
    90–92
  instructional leaders role in, 87–88
  job-embedded, 2–3, 23
  outside the classroom, 23
  sources of, 3, 88–89
  for teachers, focus on, 22–24
purpose in common, importance to the
  leadership team, 43

readiness to learn, 69–70

school
  academic program, instructional
    leaders focus on, 19
  goals and objectives, knowing and
    embracing, 116–117
  improvement plans, 117–118
  mission and vision, knowing and
    embracing the, 113–116
self-assessment, 7, 48–49

self-improvement, goal of, 50–51
self-reflection, 7–9, 36, 46–51
staff
  concerns of, when to address, 40
  meeting with, 131–132
  zip codes, importance of, 67–69
standards, focus on state-level, 18
students
  environment's effect on, 21–22
  prioritizing content over, 68
  readiness to learn, 69–70
  zip codes, importance of, 67–69

teachers
  ALT as resources for, 106–109
  anxiety, reducing, 54–55
  culturally competent, 68–69
  instructional leadership, value to,
    6–8
  potential, maximizing, 2
  professional growth and progress,
    focus on, 22–24
  shortages, 109
  skill sets and experiential back-
    grounds, focus on, 22–24
  surplus- vs. deficit-mindset,
    63–64
  zip codes, importance of, 67–69
time management, 40–41, 57–62

vision and mission, importance to the
  leadership team, 17–18, 43

zip codes, importance of, 67–69

About the Author

Baruti K. Kafele, a highly regarded urban educator in New Jersey for more than 20 years, has distinguished himself as a master teacher and a transformational school leader. As an elementary school teacher in East Orange, New Jersey, he was named East Orange School District and Essex County Public Schools Teacher of the Year, and he was a finalist for New Jersey State Teacher of the Year. As a middle and high school principal, he led the transformation of four different New Jersey urban schools, including Newark Tech, which went from a low-performing school in need of improvement to national recognition, and which was recognized by *U.S. News & World Report* as one of America's best high schools.

Kafele is one of the most sought-after school leadership experts in North America. He is the author of 14 books, including *The Aspiring Principal 50, The Assistant Principal Identity,* and his seven ASCD bestsellers: *The Assistant Principal 50, Closing the Attitude Gap, The Equity and Social Justice Education 50, Is My School a Better School Because I Lead It?, Motivating Black Males to Achieve in School and in Life, The Principal 50,* and *The Teacher 50.* He is the recipient of more than 150 educational, professional, and community awards, including the prestigious Milken Educator Award and the National Alliance of Black School Educators Hall of Fame Award. He was inducted into the East Orange, New Jersey, Hall of Fame, and the city of Dickinson, Texas, proclaimed February 8, 1998, Baruti Kafele Day. Kafele can be reached via his website, www.principalkafele.com.